ON THE BUS WITH BILL MONROE

MUSIC IN AMERICAN LIFE

A list of books in the series appears at the end of this book.

ON THE
BUS WITH BILL MONROE

My Five-Year Ride with the Father of Blue Grass

MARK HEMBREE

UNIVERSITY OF
ILLINOIS PRESS
Urbana, Chicago, and Springfield

All images are from the author's collection unless otherwise noted.

Library of Congress Cataloging-in-Publication Data
Names: Hembree, Mark, 1955– author.
Title: On the bus with Bill Monroe: my five-year ride
    with the father of blue grass / Mark Hembree.
Description: Urbana: University of Illinois Press, 2022.
    | Series: Music in American life | Includes index.
Identifiers: LCCN 2021052487 (print) | LCCN
    2021052488 (ebook) | ISBN 9780252044427
    (hardback) | ISBN 9780252086496 (paperback) |
    ISBN 9780252053412 (ebook)
Subjects: LCSH: Hembree, Mark, 1955– | Double
    bassists—United States—Biography. | Bluegrass
    musicians—United States—Biography. | Monroe,
    Bill, 1911–1996. | LCGFT: Autobiographies.
Classification: LCC ML419.H43 A3 2022 (print) | LCC
    ML419.H43 (ebook) | DDC 782.421642092/2 [B]—dc23
LC record available at https://lccn.loc.gov/2021052487
LC ebook record available at https://lccn.loc.gov/
    2021052488

To Dad, who came out of the hills and brought the music with him, and to Mom, the English teacher who never stopped correcting me.

CONTENTS

False Start Foreword   xi

Acknowledgments   xiii

PART I. INTRODUCTIONS

1. William Smith Monroe   3

2. Mark Gilbert Hembree   10

PART II. "MULESKINNER BLUES"

3. "You Just Might Have a Job"   15

4. "Shh! Shh! It's Bill!"   18

5. Monroe Enterprises   19

6. The Blue Grass Boys   21

7. Getting My Bedclothes   27

8. Learning the Vernacular   28

9. The Crucible of Chatom   31

10. Comfort Level 1   34

11. A Gentle Side of Bill   35

12. "Back Home Again in Indiana"   37

13. Uncle Birch   39

14. "Doghouse Blues"   40

15. Proper Grooming and a Tip of the Hat   41

PART III. "BREAKING IN A BRAND-NEW PAIR OF SHOES"

16. Glory Is Fleeting   47

17. The Eye   50

18. More on the Bus   51

19. Road Cuisine   52

20. A Need-to-Know Bassist   55

21. The Beer Taboo   57

22. Hangover Management   59

23. Road Journal, February 1980   60

24. Who Is That Guy?   63

25. No, Really, Who the Hell *Is* That Guy?   64

PART IV. "HEAVY TRAFFIC AHEAD"

26. Kentucky Fried Festival, Louisville   69

27. Taking My Time Capsules   71

28. John Duffey   72

29. On to Pocatello!   73

30. Rooms/No Rooms   74

31. Of Gloves and Bananas   76

32. Pushing the Bus up Cumberland Gap   77

PART V. "MY LAST DAYS ON EARTH"

33. *Master of Bluegrass*   81

34. Back in the Saddle   84

35. Monroe Hangs Tough, But It's Tough   85

PART VI. "ROCKY ROAD BLUES"

36. The Accidental Road Manager   101

37. West Coast Routing and Canadian Customs   103

38. Road Burns and the Right Rock   106

39. Rich Comes Along for the Ride   108

40. The Poker to End All Poker   110

41. Bill on Dolly, Wayne on Bill   112

42. Winning in Tahoe   113

43. Monroe Pays the Piper   114

44. The First Thing I'm Going to Do   115

45. Bean Blossom International   116

46. All Day at the Record Table   118

47. Bluegrass Death Trip   121

48. Bill Keeps Grinding   122

49. Checking on Paycheck   126

50. Mule Day, April 3, 1982, Columbia, Tennessee   128

51. Opening the Knoxville World's Fair, May 1, 1982   129

52. Uncle Birch and Southern Funerary Traditions   131

PART VII. "PRECIOUS MEMORIES"

53. Taking the Gospel Shot   135

54. July 24–27, 1982   137

55. Bridgewater, Nova Scotia, via the Emergency Room   139

56. A Record-Breaking Diss   141

57. River Ranch Resort   143

58. Bill's Birthday in Louisville   144

59. Country Hardball   146

60. McClure via Coeburn   149

61. Roll On Buddy   152

PART VIII. "OVER THE WAVES"

62. Hello, Ireland!   157

63. Bill Gets His Encore   160

64. A Wonderful School of Music   162

65. The Blue Grass Goys in Israel   163

PART IX. "LIVE AND LET LIVE"

66. Pittsburgh, Unplugged   169

67. Feats of Magic   170

68. PTL: Pass The Loot   172

69. Bluegrass and the Hippies   174

PART X. "ON AND ON"

70. Just Be Ready   179

71. Serving Notice   181

72. The Road Is Clear   183

73. Grand Ole Après   185

At Last, Thanks   187

Further Reading   193

Index   195

I started writing this book in 1979 as a Blue Grass Boy. But in 1985 I wrote a beginning that, if nothing else, showed that I still wasn't ready to write it:

> I guess I can start writing this now after five years in a different world.
>
> Early on, I wanted to write about my life as a Blue Grass Boy. My main excuse, and a good one, for not having done it was that I lacked knowledge and, thus, perspective. I was right up next to it all, yet I didn't know what was happening a lot of the time. When I first joined the band, I could barely understand what everyone was saying because of the accent and dialect. This was a handicap during the intense hazing and baiting I endured as a rookie.
>
> Now I'm off the bus and back in a van, my previous mode of travel, with a talented bunch of musicians of whom much is expected. This is how I rolled before Bill. It's not as roomy as a bus, but I'm more comfortable now. I've been back in the real world more than a year, but those five years before seem distant, as if I'd been living abroad in some foreign land. I'm only now starting to feel at home again.

So, I left it alone until now. But not all of my writing draws on forty-year-old memories. Back then, I knew my experience was significant and so I did write. I just never felt I had the perspective to write it well enough. I'm actually surprised at how much of the material I was able to keep.

What I grossly underestimated then was how quickly so much memory could dissipate. This was pointed out to me when a friend at the Country Music Hall of Fame and Museum recommended that John Rumble ask me a few questions regarding a Bill Monroe discography. I realized my memories of recording sessions only two or three years past were unreliable. So, though I sometimes cringe at some of the bright things I wrote when I was twenty-four, I've tried to preserve those notes for what they were. That's why you'll see chapters labeled "archival" (based on contemporaneous notes) and "recollected" (episodes I do remember well, notes or not). They are arranged in roughly chronological order to reflect my evolving perceptions and understanding of Bill, Kenny Baker, and the rest of the Blue Grass Boys.

This book is not a definitive work on the subject of Bill Monroe. I leave that to Monroe scholars, folklorists, and historians far more qualified than I: Neil V. Rosenberg, Charles K. Wolfe, Ralph Rinzler, Jim Rooney, John Rumble, and Tom Ewing chief among them. Also, to Thomas Adler and Jim Peva for a lot more about Bean Blossom, where Monroe held annual festivals.

I hope you've already read some of their works. I'll try to fill in as needed, but if you are already familiar with Bill Monroe, you'll enjoy this book even more. If you are a Monroe student, I hope this will provide a different view and reveal more about the man.

Several other Blue Grass Boys have written their personal recollections of working with Monroe. Not that I wasn't curious, but for years I've put off reading them because I knew I still wanted to write my own. I didn't want their memories to sneak into mine. Besides, I reasoned, why should I trust their forty-year-old memories any more than my own?

Still, those memories needed to be dusted off and sorted. For his help with that, I thank Tom Ewing for kindly providing his meticulously compiled itinerary of Monroe appearances spanning the years I worked with him.

To anyone now having an experience that might be worthy of memoirs later, I say write it down. Also heed Rosenberg's advice to me: don't throw anything away.

One more thing: other books about Monroe have dallied more in his personal life, including his love life. Some of those details illuminate his personality and character, no doubt, and in certain instances are unavoidable. But, I, who only briefly visited his home a time or two, knew very little of that.

I don't think leaving those parts out makes my account deficient. Even if I had been in the know, I don't think I'd write about it. It doesn't matter any more than Ty Cobb's evil nature or Babe Ruth's famous excesses—interesting aspects, perhaps, but not the reason Cobb, Ruth, and Bill Monroe are legends.

It's because they had game.

ACKNOWLEDGMENTS

This list can get long fast. But for this book in particular, I thank:
Chris Skinker, who has prodded me to write this book since sometime in the 1980s; George Leonard, my first and still best editor, who taught me the ropes, and Daryl Sanders, the managing editor who hired me on the word of a friend; Matthew Usher, erstwhile boss and longtime colleague, who affirmed my writing efforts at nearly every turn; Tom Ewing, whose careful and exhaustive research included a handwritten compilation of Bill Monroe's itinerary through the years I worked for him, which he kindly shared with me; Tom Adler, who advised me to stop agonizing over a cover letter and just go ahead and pitch the manuscript to the University of Illinois Press; Laurie Matheson, director of the University of Illinois Press, who took my calls, was easy to talk to, and was so supportive; Jay Feldman, a literary sharpshooter who shared his publishing experience and love of country music and baseball; John Fabke, archivist, and Thomas Goldsmith, editor and author, whose sage advice helped me put this book to bed; and Georgia Henes-Hembree, who has put up with all this and me for so many years.

ON THE BUS WITH BILL MONROE

PART I
INTRODUCTIONS

WILLIAM SMITH MONROE

Almost everyone I knew was scared of Bill Monroe. Or in awe of him. Or wary of him.

He was a big, broad-shouldered man with a countenance of hewn granite and a majestic bearing worthy of all his titles: Father of Blue Grass Music, member of the Country Music Hall of Fame, Grand Ole Opry performer since 1939.

But what made him truly intimidating was his intensity. It was right there on the surface. When he took a step back, set his shoulders, and gave that *look*, even jaded, smooth professionals began to stammer. It's not enough to say he did not suffer fools gladly. He was the same with everyone until you had done something to gain his respect.

Stone-faced . . . solemn . . . stoic . . . regal . . . intense . . . intimidating . . . driven . . . stern . . . How best to describe Bill Monroe? In his chapter of *Stars of Country Music*, Ralph Rinzler wrote, "like many charismatic but laconic artists, he was surrounded by a public unable to penetrate the body of legend which had grown up around him as a result of his silence" (202).

Southern folks came from the same place, had heard him all their lives, been where he had been, and understood his understatements. But, as Rinzler noted, northerners did not possess this innate knowledge.

If you had to choose one person most responsible for raising Bill above the regional level, it would be Rinzler. A folklorist who became director of the Smithsonian Folklife Programs, he learned mandolin in the 1950s and played in the Greenbriar Boys, who were part of the folk scene in Greenwich Village that made Bob Dylan, Joan Baez, and others famous. Rinzler's efforts brought Monroe into the folk fad of the early 1960s and, thus, into national recognition.

But Rinzler, and Mike Seeger (of the New Lost City Ramblers, and another of the great American folk chroniclers), followed Monroe around for about eight years before screwing up the courage to speak to him.

Rinzler's fascination with the Monroe culture of knowledge was ongoing. In the early 1980s, when I was in Monroe's band, Rinzler came along for a show we played at Tombstone Junction, an amusement park in Eastern

Kentucky. More outgoing in later years, Bill would open up to an audience in places where he felt comfortable, and Rinzler witnessed one of these monologues. He found it remarkable. It reinforced his observation that such audiences already understood Monroe.

This was Bill's "I will never change" speech, in which he talked about preserving his style—not adding drums, electricity, or any other "bunch of stuff." He talked about the old days when young men moved north or "to the big city" and came back "wearing their white shirts and fancy clothes," acting as if they didn't come from there. "But I will never change!" Monroe said, getting applause.

One thing that never did change was the effect his childhood had on his music—that "high, lonesome sound." He grew up near Rosine, Kentucky, the youngest of eight children. People made fun of him because he had crossed eyes, so he kept to himself. If a stranger approached the house, he would run and hide.

Poor vision hindered him at school; he couldn't see well enough to read the blackboard, and he really wanted to. His sister Bertha told me that as children they would play school, and Bill would pretend to read. Later in life, he had surgery to correct his eyes. On the road, every morning he would read the newspaper front to back. Bertha told me he was really proud of that.

I think it's safe to say he took a lot of abuse from his older brothers. It was one of the reasons he hated drunkenness, and especially beer. When he talked about it, he would recall times when his brothers would come in late from the bars and rough him up. My guess is he always associated that with the smell of beer.

As if life with his siblings was not hard enough, he lost both of his parents when he was young—his mother died when he was ten, his father six years later. Bill wound up living with his uncle Pendleton Vandiver, namesake of the song "Uncle Pen," who taught Monroe a lot about old-time fiddle. They would ride a mule to go play dances, and the mule would bring them home in the black of night, so dark "you couldn't see your hand in front of your face," Monroe recalled.

One of the jobs Monroe worked as a teen was gathering telephone poles for the phone company, single-handedly loading the logs on a wagon. Feats of strength were a regular feature of his publicity photos early in his career.

In the late 1920s, Monroe moved to Chicago—actually, Northwest Indiana—to join his brothers Birch and Charlie, who had gone north to seek their fortune in showbiz. Bill worked at a Sinclair refinery in East Chicago, Indiana, washing and stacking fifty-gallon oil drums. His brothers would come there to collect his paycheck, Bill recalled. He would sign it over and hand it to them through the fence. Dressed in suits, they would go off to town, ostensibly looking for work.

Bill, Charlie, and sometimes Birch performed together as the Monroe Brothers in the 1930s. As their recording career took off, they gained airtime and fame from the Midwest to the Carolinas. But there was a falling out, and the brothers broke up the act. Charlie continued with his own band, but it was Bill who put together a group and landed a spot on the Grand Ole Opry in 1939. His debut was sensational, and he became a lifelong member right from the start.

This was as big as the big time got. Founded in 1925, the Opry was (and still is) broadcast from Nashville on WSM. With far less competition for the airwaves in those days, it could be heard on Saturday nights across most of North America; parts of it were carried on NBC's national network. There were other country music radio shows—such as the *National Barn Dance* on WLS from Chicago, which started in 1924—but by the time Monroe hit the Opry, it was the top.

So, Bill had surpassed all his older brothers. But I don't think he ever forgave them, and it was a part of his aloof, impenetrable persona and prideful bearing. Of those days Monroe would say, "Wasn't none of them ever give me a chance."

Monroe's meteoric rise through the 1930s and 1940s had made him as big a star as any in country music. His band with Lester Flatt on guitar, Earl Scruggs on banjo, Chubby Wise on fiddle, and Howard Watts (a.k.a. Cedric Rainwater) on bass forged the original sound of bluegrass. On the Opry, when Bill rattled the rafters with his tenor, or Scruggs and his "fancy banjo" took a break, the audience screamed. Everywhere they went, Bill Monroe and his Blue Grass Boys were packing them in.

Then it all went away. The 1950s featured some of Monroe's greatest music (the harmonies with Jimmy Martin are the gold standard), but the money wasn't there. Electric instruments and drums heralded a new era in country music. And then Elvis hit.

Flatt and Scruggs had formed their own band and were vying to join the Opry. Bill tried to rally other members to keep them off, maintaining that they were merely copying him. But Flatt and Scruggs were sustained in lean times by the Martha White flour sponsorship, and it was that company's threat to pull its advertising that prompted Opry management to call a cast meeting to announce that Flatt and Scruggs would be made members, over Monroe's objections.

Bill had no such business acumen. Why should he? He was already a star. But his success had suddenly flown. In years to come, there were times Bill slept in the car so the boys in the band could have rooms.

When I met Don Reno, the banjo player who succeeded Scruggs in Monroe's band, he asked me how I liked working for Bill—then laughed when I shrugged, unwilling to go on record. Bill hadn't always been so tough, he said. When Monroe was riding high, he was more easygoing. If they had a flat tire on the way to a show, Bill would pull out the baseball gloves and want to have some catch. After a while someone might look at his watch and say, well, we're running late, guess we'd better get this flat fixed, but Bill would be in no hurry. They'll wait, he'd say, and he was right. People who were lined up around the block to get in wouldn't mind a late start.

In those days, admission was taken in nickels, dimes, and quarters. (Bill recalled how people complained when the price went up to twenty-five cents.) At the end of a trip, the car sat back on its haunches from the weight of all the coins in the trunk. To pay the band, Bill took his share and then scooped the change into four roughly equal piles. It was never counted. And that was your pay for the week, Reno said.

Monroe watched from not so far away as Flatt and Scruggs's fame eclipsed his own. Holding fast to the style he believed had been stolen from him, unwilling to make such compromises as taking a bit part in a hokey TV sitcom (as Flatt and Scruggs did in *The Beverly Hillbillies*), Bill gained a reputation as an ascetic—a stern disciplinarian who could be cruel to his band members, and a purist who labeled any divergent style of bluegrass "no kind of music, that ain't no part of nothin'."

You can see that look on his face in a lot of photos from the 1950s and 1960s. Whatever else was going on around him in the picture, Bill still looked angry and aggrieved. The defensive reticence of his childhood seemed to have returned.

Credit Rinzler for the emergence of Monroe in folk music narratives up north. But it wasn't easy, and it took more than one try.

When *Sing Out!* reported in 1962 that Scruggs had become "the undisputed master of Bluegrass music," Rinzler sought to set the record straight. But that year, in an exchange described by Neil V. Rosenberg in *Bluegrass: A History*, when Rinzler asked Monroe for an interview, Bill said, "If you want to know about bluegrass music, ask Louise Scruggs," and then walked away (182).

Rinzler would have known the story of Monroe's ongoing feud with Flatt and Scruggs. He may not have known Monroe was aware that Earl's wife, Louise Scruggs, had arranged for the Greenbriar Boys (with Rinzler) to be guests on the Opry. That would account for the snub.

Assigning guilt by association was not unusual for Bill. If you were chumming around with someone he didn't like and wasn't talking to, he would let you know it (before he stopped talking to you, too).

Once Monroe finally did grant Rinzler an audience, not surprisingly, Bill proved a tough interview. But when he read the published piece and saw the high regard in which he was held by Rinzler, their relationship became "one of unquestioning confidence and trust," Rinzler wrote in *Stars of Country Music* (205). It was the very beginning of a long thaw.

So, at the height of the folk fad, when the world came calling again, new fans of bluegrass music soon learned that many of the top bluegrass bands were stocked with former Blue Grass Boys, and that the teachers they were taking lessons from regarded Monroe as a giant. And Bill, now older and gray but still straight backed and broad shouldered, looked every bit the part. He was as strong as ever.

But he was still a hard man to know. He preferred to say less, not more, like most country folks in the South: tight lipped, guarded, not volunteering information, cards always close to the vest.

Bill mellowed years later. Country music historian Bill Malone told me he thought Monroe became a nicer person after he stopped thinking everyone was stealing his music. He came to accept and enjoy his role as patriarch.

Along the way, he grew more tolerant—but not a lot. "That ain't no kind of music," was his usual assessment of "progressive" bands, although if they were successful enough he might admit, "They've got their own style, and the college kids likes 'em."

And though he was a purist, he did hear other styles and used whatever he could from them, trying out ideas. But onstage he felt obligated to sound as he always had, and thought that fans would be disappointed otherwise.

Still, that didn't necessarily mean being static or playing it safe. Early in my time with him, he was trying to coach me—or at least tell me I wasn't getting it. "You've got to get down and study the music," he said.

Looking for clues, I told him I had heard his music all my life. My dad had a lot of his records, and I had listened to his style and what other bass players had done with him.

"But I've had a lot of sorry bass players!" he said.

I took that to mean he didn't want me to count on what I'd heard on records. And I came to realize that although his style was well known and often imitated, he expected you to bring something of your own to it. Don't copy it. *Play* it.

Bill never could verbally articulate or explain his style. When he tried, it was, as Peter Rowan put it, in "bluegrass code." He left you guessing on how to do it right. But he would surely let you know if you were doing it wrong—and even stop the band midsong for a major offense.

If he was angry at you, for whatever reason, he could make you miserable. His rhythm was so powerful that he could ever-so-subtly, without breaking stride, make it nigh impossible for you to play. It was like running, being knocked a little off balance and, as you recovered, being nudged again in a different direction and set reeling again.

This might go on for days or weeks. Then, about the time you began to believe you'd lost all musical sense, he would get right with you and make you feel like you had your chops back.

But it was never soothing. Being right there in sync with him was like grabbing a live wire—exciting, but not really pleasant.

Always entertaining, though. Like the greats of the vaudeville era, Monroe could dance as well as sing and play. Even in his seventies, he could bust some moves. He could glide sideways, like James Brown, or back, like Michael Jackson. With his show savvy, imposing physique, athletic grace, and undeniable charisma, he dominated a stage. Even if an audience didn't know him at all, they could tell he was a big deal and must be famous somewhere.

I didn't fully appreciate the scope of his music until I saw more of its influence. The top bluesmen certainly knew him (you can hear Monroe licks in B.B. King's solos). Rock and rollers knew him—there's a whole side of Sun recordings where Elvis impersonates him while trying out Monroe tunes. (Of course, Elvis did record "Blue Moon of Kentucky." And Monroe is in the Rock and Roll Hall of Fame.) Even Ella Fitzgerald! In an unusual pairing, we opened a show for her at a Kentucky Fried Chicken national convention in Las Vegas. "An honor to meet you," said the First Lady of Song to Monroe.

Still, business was never his strong suit. His stubborn—some might say foolish—pride often got in the way. Jim Rooney, music producer and author of *Bossmen: Bill Monroe and Muddy Waters*, told me a story of how he and Rinzler attempted to negotiate a better recording deal for Monroe. They had been working through it with Bill, but when they showed up for the big meeting, carrying briefcases and ready to roll, Monroe was already there to tell them he had made his agreement, they'd shook hands on it, and that was good enough for him.

At that point in the story, Rooney threw up his hands. "And that was it for me," he said.

Moreover, schmoozing and networking were not in Monroe's nature. He was already as famous as he had ever wanted to be.

For example, we were playing a festival somewhere in New Jersey one afternoon, and someone sent word that Robert Duvall was there and would like to meet Monroe. Bill didn't know who he was. Blake Williams was the banjo player then, and we told Bill that Duvall was a big movie star, and it might be a good thing to meet him.

Just after the show, a storm came up and rained out the rest of the festival. We got soaked getting back to the bus, but once there we could see a black limo parked nearby, engine running. That must be Duvall, Blake and I thought. Perhaps one of us mentioned this to Bill. But he was more interested in getting down the road and finding a place to eat. So we rolled out of there and left Duvall sitting in the rain. Blake and I looked at each other and said nothing.

This was around the time Duvall was working on *Tender Mercies*, a film about a recovering country music singer for which Duvall won an Oscar as best actor. Might he have been doing some deep background and research for his role? Was he there to ask Monroe to do a cameo in the film? We'll never know. It didn't matter to Bill.

Were there other such missed opportunities along the way? Certainly. Could Bill have risen above the stature he achieved? Probably. But could it ever have been any other way? Probably not.

As Rinzler wrote so well, "A man more easily persuaded would likely not have succeeded in so formidable an undertaking as bucking the cultural and economic tide of the country music industry" (219).

Or, as Monroe often said, "I will never change."

I was born in Chicago in 1955 and grew up in Appleton, Wisconsin, the hometown of Harry Houdini, Edna Ferber, Joe McCarthy, Rocky Bleier, Willem Dafoe, and the world's first hydroelectric plant.

But how do you grow up near Green Bay and wind up in Bill Monroe's band? Dumb luck, mostly, and early musical exposure. My mother was from Topeka, Kansas; she played the organ and liked classical and popular music. My father was from Waynesville, North Carolina; he played the radio and the stereo, and it was old-time fiddle, bluegrass, and western swing.

Dad was a sales rep, and on Saturday nights when he was off the road, he would cook hamburgers and try to tune in the Grand Ole Opry (never a sure thing in northeastern Wisconsin). I sat on his lap, listening to the radio hiss and pop, and soaking up the sweet smell of gin, onions, and aftershave, while he talked about the music—how Roy Acuff's voice projected ("he bounces it off the back wall"), how the Dobro complemented the other instruments ("listen to how he builds a platform under them"), and how a fiddle could cut through steel like a welding torch.

"The only thing that cuts better than a good fiddle is a bad fiddle," he said.

If he thought the kids were sleeping too late, he'd crank up the stereo and play Monroe or Acuff. Often, it was Monroe singing "Were You There." I'd get up to make it stop.

There were five kids in the family, and we all took music lessons. I sang in choir and played trombone in the school band, but nothing stuck until Dad gave me a Gibson J-50 guitar when I was in seventh grade.

I spent more and more time with it, and it wasn't long before I discovered girls really liked it, which of course made me want to play more. I could fake Leo Kottke and John Fahey well enough to get gigs at college coffeehouses before I was old enough to have a driver's license. My sister drove me to the gigs.

Once in a while Dad would host picking parties and have friends over who played bluegrass. He would try to get me to join in, but I was too cool for that. I would oblige for a few tunes, then excuse myself and go do something more important (like, I don't know what).

In 1972, everyone played guitar. So I took orchestra class to get a bass. I played Crosby, Stills, Nash & Young stuff in a band, but we'd be drowned out in a bar.

Then I saw a bluegrass band called the Monroe Doctrine playing in the rathskeller at Lawrence University. Though I had seen bluegrass before, these were young, hip guys, and they were blowing this college crowd away. It was an epiphany: here was an acoustic band with more chops than any band I had played in, three-part harmonies, and it was rocking the place.

I resolved to find or start a bluegrass band. And then, because of Dad, I found the music was already in my head. I was ahead of the locals.

Somehow, bluegrass had become popular with young folks. Maybe it was the acoustic stuff coming out at the time (the Beatles' *Rubber Soul* album, Lovin' Spoonful, pop folk, etc.), or maybe it was the Flying Burrito Brothers (formed in 1969 by migrating Byrds Gram Parsons and Chris Hillman). The same year, Bob Dylan released his *Nashville Skyline* album.

Then, in 1972, the movie *Deliverance* featured "Dueling Banjos" (actually "Feudin' Banjos" by Arthur "Guitar Boogie" Smith, for which he sued and won due credit). A banjo instrumental went to number 1 on *Billboard*'s Easy Listening chart! And that year the Nitty Gritty Dirt Band brought out *Will the Circle Be Unbroken*, a triple album that made cross-genre music an intramural event. The long-haired hippie singers of "Mr. Bojangles" booked Nashville country and bluegrass stalwarts for the session: Acuff (with Pete "Bashful Brother Oswald" Kirby on Dobro), Merle Travis, Doc Watson, Maybelle Carter, Earl Scruggs (but not Lester Flatt), Vassar Clements, Norman Blake, Junior Huskey, and Jimmy Martin (but not Bill Monroe).

It was too bad Monroe shunned that bunch of hippie boys, because the album sold like hotcakes and gave everyone's career a pretty good bump— especially Doc, Vassar, and Jimmy, along with a bunch of kids like me who couldn't believe bluegrass was on the radio. Even Monroe would benefit from the buzz.

All of a sudden, bluegrass music was cool. There was (ex–Blue Grass Boy) Byron Berline, fiddling on Stephen Stills's *Manassas* album. And here was Jerry Garcia of the Grateful Dead, recording *Old & In the Way* with Vassar and Peter Rowan (both former Blue Grass Boys) and David Grisman, who had been taught mandolin by Ralph Rinzler and had earned his traditional bluegrass stripes with Red Allen and the Kentuckians before joining the hip scene on the West Coast. Bluegrass was big on campus.

I graduated from high school with no desire to proceed to college, worked a few months as a Pinkerton guard on the third shift at a wire mill (because I could play guitar between rounds), and saved my money to go bum around Europe.

But the day my passport arrived in the mail, I got a call to join a band in Green Bay. It was a full-time bluegrass band with a weekly radio show. My first pro gig! Dad said Mom hung the place in black. Looked like I wasn't going to med school. Europe could wait.

The *Glenmore Country Barndance* was an hour-long live program on WGEE, the CBS affiliate in Green Bay. With an eighty-mile radius, the broadcast covered a lot of territory. Live radio is where I learned one of the most important rules in showbiz: *don't stop.*

Looking back, I see how little a twenty-two-year-old actually knows. I had no idea of how well-off we were for a bluegrass band. Each guy was making $200 to $250 per week, not bad in 1976. But I went away to try to get famous. It would be a long time before I saw that kind of pay again, even with Monroe.

I wound up in Denver with a later version of the Monroe Doctrine, that band I'd seen at Lawrence University. I had met Georgia, my future wife, in Green Bay, and I had not considered that she would come with me to Colorado until she asked me why not. Then it was her parents' turn to be dismayed— their daughter was dropping out of college to move out to Denver with a bluegrass musician, whatever the hell that was.

Times were lean. The band was ahead of its time, long before anything called jamgrass. Tony Trischka filled in on banjo for a couple of tours. (He was telling us about this fourteen-year-old student of his in New York City who had come to him playing Charlie Parker solos—Béla Fleck.)

But there wasn't a lot of work. Georgia and I went on food stamps and ate a lot of noodle casseroles. Then, about the time the band was starting to take off, it broke up.

Georgia and I moved back to Milwaukee, where she waitressed at a ritzy restaurant downtown. I became service manager at a waterbed store, working for a man who had legally changed his name to Japhy Ryder, a Jack Kerouac character. It's the only job I've ever had where I could call in *well.* "You know, Japhy, it's a beautiful day and the Brewers are playing this afternoon. I just feel too damn good to come in!"

We found a nice apartment in Bay View and settled in for what would be a short stay.

PART II
"MULESKINNER BLUES"

(recollected)

What better way to entertain an out-of-state visitor to Milwaukee than to offer a trip to Mukwonago? It's actually a scenic drive, and there was a big bluegrass festival going on there when my friend Jon Pushkin swung by on a vacation in June 1979.

I had met Pushkin, a jazz and swing guitarist and singer from New Jersey, when he was part of a musical crowd that revolved around the Denver Folklore Center. In the days after I left Colorado, he and Monroe Doctrine mandolinist Wayne Beezley toured as the Baby Watson Brothers. Pushkin was (and still is) a fellow well met, retaining his Joisey accent to go with a quick wit.

Although we had many mutual friends, Pushkin was not hip to the traditional bluegrass scene. As we stood gazing at Jimmy Martin's motor home—its sides covered with a crudely painted mural of raccoons and possums—Jimmy emerged in full stage regalia: bright red suit, white shirt, white belt and shoes, and a brocade cowboy hat.

"Look at him!" Pushkin howled and bent over laughing. I urged restraint. "Jon, he might look funny but he's not deaf," I said, turning away.

As for looks, we two were letting our freak flags fly—Pushkin with a shoulder-length bush of curls, me with wavy red hair nearly to my waist. Not a look you'd find at a camp meeting in the South.

About then, friends from the Piper Road Spring Band ran up to tell me there was an opening in Bill Monroe's band. They had been at Monroe's Bean Blossom festival the week before, where Randy Davis had just ended a five-year term playing bass. Raymond Huffmaster, a mountainous good ol' boy from Mississippi, was filling in. But he was a guitar player.

OK, there was an opening. But what of it? I couldn't approach Monroe looking like I did. Bill Monroe and his Blue Grass Boys wore suits, ties, and cowboy hats. Hair was off the collar.

Yet Pushkin goaded me. "C'mon, man! Whaddaya got to lose? Go play a few tunes with the Father of Blue Grass! Why not?"

So I tied my hair back as best I could and went to Monroe to ask for an audition. As I spoke, I could see him eying my ponytail. "Bill, I've seen your band many times and I know they don't wear hair like this. I can get this cut in a second. It doesn't matter to me."

Monroe nodded. "We've had a long drive and we're awful tired," he said. "Could you come around tomorrow?" I told him I would see him in the morning before the gospel show. "That'd be fine," he said.

I felt funny about going after someone else's job, though, so I went to talk to Huffmaster and asked him whether it was true that he was just filling in. Yeah, I ain't no bass player, he said, but he looked at that ponytail and said I'd better clean up good. Monroe wasn't about to hire no hippie boy.

Well, now Pushkin had to stay another day to see what happened.

When we got back to Milwaukee, Georgia took one last picture of me before her sister-in-law gave me a haircut—not exactly whitewalls around the ears, but off the collar.

The next morning, Pushkin and I drove back out to the festival. There was no time before the gospel set, though, and Monroe put me off until the afternoon show. That wound up being an all-day wait, as Monroe would close the show.

Finally, as the band gathered backstage before their last set, I got my audience with His Billness. He asked what I could play, and I suggested a fiddle number, "Road to Columbus." Kenny Baker abruptly launched into it, and away we went—and we started to groove. I couldn't believe I was playing with *Kenny Baker*! I glanced at Butch Robins as he hitched a banjo riff to an ascending bass line, and I thought I even saw Monroe smile a little as he turned to Baker and said, "That's a dance beat there." I didn't know whether he liked my rhythm or they were amused by my bouncing around. (I had not yet adopted the Blue Grass Boys' steadfast, stationary stance.)

I knew Monroe's bass players usually sang bass in the quartet, and maybe a little baritone, so when he asked whether I could sing I told him I could take the bass on "A Beautiful Life," a gospel song with a bass lead on the chorus and answering parts on the verses (minimizing my need to know more lyrics). I sang that well enough. And then it was time for the band to go on.

I thanked Monroe and walked out to the top of the hill to watch the show, Pushkin chattering all along about how I had aced the test.

After the show, Butch came trotting up the hill toward their bus. He said they were going to blast out of there as soon as they could, but if I had a business card or something I should give it to the old man. "You just might have a job," he said, and hurried off.

Pushkin threw his arms wide and yelled like *Captain Kangaroo*'s Banana Man, "Woooowww!" I jotted my numbers on a card and walked toward Monroe's bus, where he stood greeting fans and signing autographs.

As I walked toward Monroe I was cut off by a familiar old-timer—Bob Krenke, a regular at my dad's picking parties when I was growing up. *No! Bob!* I thought, but here he was, in standard-issue checkered shirt, western belt, and cowboy hat, carrying a banjo. He got to Monroe before I could.

I didn't know that Bob had been watching my audition from a distance. Now he had come to provide a job reference. He shook Monroe's hand and introduced himself: Bob Krenke, postmaster of Dale, Wisconsin. Monroe said he was pleased to meet him (in small towns, the postmaster holds a high position).

Bob said, "Bill, I just wanted to tell you I've known this young man since he was knee high. I've known his father for many years, and he's a good man, an honest man. I've always thought this boy's got talent, and I think he'd make a good man for your band."

Monroe nodded, shook his hand again, and thanked him. Then he turned to me. I handed him my card and told him he could reach me at work during the day. Playing with him would be a great privilege, I added. I guess he agreed. He shook my hand and got on the bus, the door slammed shut, the engine spooled up, and they pulled out.

Bob, Pushkin, and I stood there in the dust, watching the bus go.

When I got home I told Georgia what happened. "Oh, great," she groused. "Where does *he* live?"

"Tennessee," I said, "Nashville, I guess."

"Great!" she said. We had just moved back to Milwaukee from Denver and had a nice place. All her family lived nearby.

"Don't worry," I said. "It's just an audition. There are plenty of pickers in Nashville. It's not like I got the job."

"Oh, you'll get the job. Great! Just *great!*" she said, and went off to sulk.

4 "SHH! SHH! IT'S BILL!"

(recollected)

Pushkin went on with his vacation travels, and I went back to my job at Land & Sky Waterbeds in Milwaukee.

The store manager, Smokey Kirton, was a South Carolina gal who knew her bluegrass. After I told her about the audition, whenever the phone rang she'd say, "Shh! Shh! It's Bill!"

Then one afternoon about two weeks later, the phone rang, and I called out, "Shh! It's Bill!" But this time, for some reason, Smokey darted over to the radio and turned it off.

I answered the phone, then looked at her, pointing at the phone and mouthing, "It's Bill!" She sat down on a nearby bed and put her hands to her face.

"When can you be down in Nashville?" Monroe asked.

"Well, I can check the flights. I might be able to get a plane out tonight," I said.

Bill might have chuckled. "Uh, how would two weeks be?"

"Yessir, that'd be fine."

Monroe said, "Now, I want a man who will work hard and be on time, and I want a sober man. And then we'll just see how it goes from there."

"I'll do my best," I said. "I'm thrilled to have the chance. I'll do the best I can."

"Well, alright then," Monroe said.

After he gave me his number and address, I said, "OK, I'll see you in two weeks." I was hoping he'd say more.

He didn't. "Alright," he said and hung up.

I hung up and stared at the phone.

Smokey leapt up screaming and hugged me as I repeated, "I don't believe it. I just don't believe it."

The next day I called Dad to tell him I had a new job. With Bill Monroe.

There was a long pause. "Bill Monroe? *The* Bill Monroe?"

"Yeah," I said. "You know, old guy, plays mandolin, sings tenor, Grand Ole Opry? That guy."

Another long pause. Then, "Goddamn! Well, glory be! I'll be goddamned!"

After we hung up, he went down to Gloudemans department store and bought six short-sleeve white shirts and a pair of black dress shoes. He knew I'd need them.

MONROE ENTERPRISES   5

(archival)

Bill said to be at his office at noon.

The "office" out on Dickerson Pike was a square two-room trailer, clad in blue aluminum, with a dilapidated house trailer parked to one side and a gravel lot out front. Two railroad ties served as parking blocks.

The inside was carpeted in bluish shag, dirty and matted. There were a couple of chairs, a couch upholstered in vinyl that was splitting at the arms, and a desk behind which sat the secretary, Carolyn, Bill's ex-wife and the mother of his son, James. Her wig was in worse shape than the carpet, its worn and faded base stretched over her pate like a shower cap. She wore thick, garish makeup.

"He ain't here," she said, eying me indifferently.

"I'm Mark Hembree, the new bass player," I said. She shrugged. None of her business. "Will he be back soon?" I asked. Another shrug. "He's gone to lunch," she said.

"May I wait for him here?" I asked. No answer. I didn't have much choice. I had been dropped there, and my ride was gone.

I spent the next few long minutes surveying the offices of Monroe Enterprises. The other room in the trailer looked like Bill's office, the desk covered with papers, the door between propped open with a wooden wedge. On the walls were various certificates of achievement and recognition, along with carved and wood-burned plaques bearing his name—obviously works of art presented to him by fans. A few copies of *Bluegrass Unlimited* magazine lay about. I found that surprising, somehow. It seemed odd that the Father of Blue Grass would bother with a trade/fan magazine.

Crunching gravel announced the arrival of Bill's sky blue Cadillac. He stepped through the door, and I rose to shake his hand. He greeted me in nearly the same distracted manner as Carolyn. I asked what time we would depart. Not for a while, he said.

Then he laid down on the couch, turned his back, and went to sleep. I sat in a chair across from him and pretended to read, watching the great Bill Monroe take a nap.

The rest of the band arrived at 6 p.m., wondering why we had to leave so early for a show the next night in Staunton, Virginia, only eight hours away. I improved their mood by telling them I had been there since noon.

That night, as we rode east on I-40, I sat up front for a long time trying to absorb the reality that I was riding Bill Monroe's bus as a member of the band.

When I awoke around dawn the next morning—or so I thought—we were parked on a county fairgrounds surrounded by rusty, dew-covered vintage farm implements. I realized no one was around. They had all gone off to breakfast.

It was another very long day for me. The hours dragged on, made longer and stranger by the fact that nobody talked to me. Everyone got rides into town to eat and kill time, while I sat, uninvited, gazing at the livestock and farm implements.

It wasn't until later in the day that food became available on the grounds. I spent the hours reading and wondering, without asking, whether we might rehearse. Shining shoes was one of the few activities I shared with the band.

I had yet to play with Monroe since my brief audition a few weeks before, but the day passed with no rehearsal, no instructions, and little to no conversation.

Finally, around 7:30 P.M., the Boys began dressing for the show. I got dressed, carried my bass to a backstage room, and tuned up. We warmed up with two or three tunes, and then it was time to go on.

Just like that, I was a Blue Grass Boy. I got crossed up a couple of times, but I guess I did OK. Later, Butch would laugh and say no one could have come into that gig any colder.

After the show, I put away my bass and helped stow the records concession. Bill was standing in the door of the bus, greeting fans. It began to rain. I stood by silently until the shower became a downpour, then bolted through the door, slithering around Bill and up the steps.

He turned around and looked at me quizzically. "Mom always told me I ought to have sense enough to come in out of the rain," I said. He gave a half smile and turned back to his conversation, while the rest of the boys looked at me and laughed, shaking their heads.

I guess he wanted to see how long I would stand out there getting soaked before I did something about it.

THE BLUE GRASS BOYS   6

(recollected)

None of these stories would be all they should be if you don't know at least a little about the characters. This leads me to some of the most difficult writing in this book—introducing the Blue Grass Boys as they were when I played in the band.

When Monroe hired me, none of the Boys were particularly happy with his choice. Randy Davis had been the bass player for five years, and he was a solid musician who made everyone's work easier. He also was a nice guy and well liked.

I preferred to think Monroe recognized my talent when he gave me the job, but I also wondered how much truth there was to the idea that I was hired because Randy and I wore close to the same size. Bill wouldn't have to buy new suits.

The dangers of writing about the Blue Grass Boys in summary are mainly those of omission—and I have omitted a lot, with good reason. I don't think any of the differences I had with my bandmates are of much interest, even to those who know the principals in the conflicts. Rather than compile a tally of slights, fights, or grievances, I've chosen to gloss those over. Sure, I've got stories about them. I know they have stories about me. I will spare you nearly all of them unless they're too funny to leave out.

Short of detailed biographical sketches that would do each one of them justice—or, more likely, some injustice—I must tell at least a little bit about the bandmates I spent so many hours with, hearing their stories, listening to them snore and belch, sharing their adventures and misadventures. It's impossible to write very much about riding the bus with Monroe without them.

Time heals (nearly) all wounds. It's even more true that time wounds all heels. We should all be even by now. And so, risking that equilibrium, and with apologies to all for the great things about them I have failed to mention, here they are—or, as Bill often said at the start of a show, "The Blue Grass Boys are ready to go."

KENNY BAKER

"The greatest fiddler in bluegrass music" is how Monroe always introduced Baker, and in the twenty-five years Baker was in the band no one ever thought Bill was exaggerating. "Melodic, fluid style" is how the *New York Times* referred to his playing in its obituary, and that is apt—especially *fluid*.

I will always remember the first time I saw him play. It was late in the evening at the Bean Blossom festival, a perfect summer night in Indiana, and Baker was playing "Jerusalem Ridge" to a spellbound crowd. "Look at him!" my classically trained friend whispered. "Look at his bowing. His wrist is like water!" I know a lot of classical players came to our shows to see that right hand and that violin—rumored to be a Guarnerius, although Kenny neither confirmed nor denied that to me.

In liner notes for the album *Kenny Baker Plays Bill Monroe*, Douglas "Ranger Doug" Green wrote the best description of Baker I've ever read:

> Ornery and irascible, cheerful and charming, demanding musically yet frequently found jamming all night with sleepy, mediocre musicians, stubborn and bull-headed, witty and warm, Kenny Baker, like bluegrass music itself, is complex, contradictory, and deep.

Sometimes Baker reminded me of Popeye, muttering and all, sleeves rolled up, a Lucky Strike dangling from his lip while he dealt cards and carried on a constant chatter.

Indeed, he was a US Navy man in World War II. Enlistment was his ticket out of the Eastern Kentucky coal mines. He served in the USO and traveled the Pacific theater with small combos playing popular tunes.

This experience was an essential part of his rare musical mélange. From Jenkins, Kentucky, he had the traditional Appalachian fiddler's background of tunes passed down from his forebears, but he also had an ear for swing and jazz. He could play that big-band sock rhythm on guitar, chords stating the melody, and excellent fingerstyle as well. On fiddle, he could saw a breakdown neatly in half, but he could also bow with the sweet, polished tone of Stéphane Grappelli and no trace of an edge or scratch.

He could be ornery. Like a true mountaineer, he didn't volunteer much information. "By God, son, the best piece of advice I'll ever give you is don't let nobody know your goddamn business," he said. That held true with me, anyway—I never visited his home, never met any of his friends outside of those who attended shows, and tried to stay out of his way. I guess he tolerated my playing, although not without complaints. I was willing to take it, though—I knew I didn't have his talent and never would. I would never have his ears.

Of course, no one would. They were a prominent part of his anatomy, and you could see them move with the music. I don't know who got away with it first, but someone nicknamed him "Flop" (short for the tune "Flop-Eared Mule"), and it stuck. I never had the brass to call him that myself. But if he rode me too hard I'd call him Yoda. He was pissed off when he found out what that meant, and he confronted me. I turned him by saying, "You never heard me call you Flop, did you?"

Late one night on the bus, I got up from my bunk and went up front, where Baker was riding shotgun. I knew the driver was from Georgia, and I asked him what a eucalyptus tree looked like. He described it, and Baker asked why I wanted to know. I've been reading this book, I said, and it mentions this tree a lot. I was just trying to picture it in my mind.

"What book is that?" he asked. "Oh, it's called *Tobacco Road*," I said.

"Erskine Caldwell, right?" he said. "Wrote *God's Little Acre*, didn't he? Haven't read that in years."

I was stunned. The only books I'd ever seen him read were by Louis L'Amour and Zane Grey. I shared that story with (ex–Blue Grass Boy) Bob Fowler, and he asked whether I'd ever been out to Kenny's house. Never had. You should see it, Bob said, wall-to-wall books on every subject you can imagine, history, psychology, you name it.

Uh huh. Don't let nobody know your damned business.

WAYNE LEWIS

Wayne was a powerful singer and rhythm guitarist. Cutting a handsome figure, broad-shouldered and barrel-chested, he rivaled Monroe in physique and was second in command onstage, stepping up to the mike if Bill was delayed by a broken string or an autograph seeker. He was also Bill's bag man, entrusted to deal with promoters and collect the pay. "He's got good judgment," Bill would say.

Cowboy boots were standard stage wear for Wayne, and he looked natural under a Stetson. He liked western novels, too, usually Louis L'Amour, and the western-noir descriptions, like "opening the ball" for the start of a fight. Fittingly, Butch nicknamed him "Durango."

Wayne came from Sandy Hook, Kentucky. Although he wasn't really a mountaineer—more from southern Ohio, around Portsmouth—he swore allegiance to the South, often telling audiences the Confederacy never lost the Civil War, because Southerners took over Michigan, Indiana, and Ohio. He was fond of all the southern sayings, such as "busier than a one-armed paperhanger," or "nervous as a long-tailed cat in a room full of rocking chairs." One of my favorites was, "What's that got to do with the price of eggs in China?"

Having been a trucker many years before, he was often called on to relieve the hired bus driver. He wasn't crazy about the double duty, but he performed it cheerfully, yakking up a storm on the CB radio. His handle was "Colt 45. Drink it or shoot it." He would point to highway caution signs and say, "Snake in the road," or, "Watch out for flying deer."

Gregarious, with a ready smile, he never met anyone he didn't think he could charm. This included all manner of law enforcement. One morning around dawn he was pulled over for speeding. When the trooper got to the driver's side, Wayne slid the window open, grinned, and called out, "Mornin'!"

The trooper asked if he know how fast he was going.

"No, sir."

"I had you at about seventy-eight."

"Is that all? You should have seen me a while ago!"

"I'm gonna have to write you a ticket."

"I don't blame you, but go right ahead. We're runnin' late."

The trooper asked where we were headed and whether Bill was aboard, and finally gave Wayne a warning. Just hold it down, he said. Wayne said he would, all the way to the county line. This got a smile out of the trooper. Then Wayne said, "Can I shoot your gun?"

The trooper laughed and walked back to his car.

BUTCH ROBINS

Butch had been with Monroe for a couple of years before I joined the band, and he was the most communicative of all the Boys when I came in. Six years my senior, he was the closest to me in age. He had a patina of hipness, having played with New Grass Revival and Leon Russell (in addition to traditional cred, having been around bluegrass music from childhood on, and playing with Charlie Moore, Jim & Jesse, and Wilma Lee & Stoney Cooper).

After I auditioned for Bill, it was Butch, hustling back to the bus, who paused to tell me I might actually have a shot. And it was he who retrieved Randy Davis's suits from the dry cleaner's and presented them to me, along with advice on upkeep and their usual rotation (it wasn't always easy to find out what color we would be wearing for the next show). I owed him a lot early on for all the advice and mentoring.

He was probably the best read of all the Boys (with the possible exception of Baker, who actually concealed it). And, if he was in the mood, he could be every bit as charming as he was owlish when he was in no mood.

Voluble and mercurial, he offered plenty of philosophizing to go with the more solid musical advice, from the realm of Zen or Sufi or whatever he was reading at the time. That I could take or leave, but he was an absolutist when it came to things he deemed proven and true.

Still, we got along well enough. And I really liked his banjo playing—great sense of rhythm, a full, pleasant tone, and an ability to play melodies eloquently without being flashy.

And it's important for me to say that he taught me a lot about Bill and the Monroe mystique. That certainly led to a greater understanding in a much shorter time than it would have taken me on my own.

BLAKE WILLIAMS

There is a kindness in people who immediately put you at ease, and it's one of Blake's great attributes. It works in tandem with his classic, dry sense of humor—he's the Bob and Ray of bluegrass.

Blake's from Sparta, Tennessee—Lester Flatt's hometown—and he actually did play in Flatt's band. Before that, he had been a local radio DJ and then toured with Bobby Smith. So he'd been around, yet never far away from Monroe. When Butch left in 1981, Blake, who was playing with Bill's son, James Monroe, was an easy choice.

I was determined to make him feel more welcome than I had been when I joined. Becoming a Blue Grass Boy is a nervous business, and the Boys had not made it easy on me. Monroe enjoyed the constant needling, and he was pretty good at it himself, so he egged them on. I got through it, but it wore me thin. A friend I hadn't seen in a while asked me why my jaw looked swollen. It was from gritting my teeth; I hadn't noticed until he mentioned it, but I could see it in pictures.

I knew right off that Blake and I would get along. It was great to have a contemporary (he's a year younger than me), as well as someone who was part of the southern culture yet articulate and forthcoming.

He could explain things to me—even coach me on my accent or tell me what the hell some country feller had just said, like the time at a truck stop just east of Memphis where I stepped off the bus and the pump attendant said, "Yow wont suhdaze."

Huh?

"Yeah, fill 'er up," Blake said, and we started walking toward the restaurant. "What did that guy say?" I asked. "He said, 'Do y'all want some diesel?'" What? That's what he said? Really? Blake, laughing, allowed as how people in West Tennessee talked funny.

Blake joined not long after the *Master of Bluegrass* album was recorded, and Bill, naturally, wanted to play that stuff on shows. All those mandolin instrumentals, all at once, was a tall order for any banjo player. (Butch called them tongue twisters.) Blake could sure enough power a breakdown—absolutely a must in Flatt's band—but now he had to pick his way through all these quirky things. I coached him on a tune or two, at least as I knew them, but I quit doing that when Monroe overheard us one night and started making fun of it.

Blake got through that, though, without getting mad at me, and we became chums as well as roomies. Road life became much less onerous. We had a lot of laughs.

GETTING MY BEDCLOTHES

7

(recollected)

In my earliest days in Nashville, before I had a car or an apartment, truck stops were my ports of call. Truckstops of America (TA) were the best, offering a retail selection of toiletries, automotive and office supplies, snacks, and souvenirs.

As we were parked at a TA in Nashville, about to leave on a trip, Baker asked whether I had any bedclothes. No, I just sleep in my shorts and T-shirt, I said. No, son, I mean *bedclothes*. For your bed.

Oh. *Sheets*. For my bunk. It hadn't even occurred to me.

You can probably get you a set here, he advised. I did and put them on my mattress in a lower bunk over the rear wheels.

Off-road lodging was another matter. Shortly before my coming to Nashville, a former bandmate had referred me to Alan O'Bryant. His hospitality was extraordinarily gracious, considering he didn't know me at all, but I had definitely overstayed my welcome. Baker knew a woman who ran a small motel just up Dickerson Pike from Bill's office. The Astro Motel was cheap enough, and the woman who ran it let me defray a little of the cost by doing some mowing and clipping around the place.

Bill hadn't yet said whether I was still on trial or had the job, and I hadn't asked. This had been my status for about a month when we traveled to Upstate New York to play at the Berkshire Mountains Blue Grass Festival (later called Winterhawk). I was glad to be back up north and see a few acquaintances from my previous music life. Béla Fleck was there, along with a friend of his from Boston, bassist Mark Schatz.

Schatz asked me about how I had gotten the job. So I told him my story, how I patiently waited until Bill was ready, and what I played in the audition. Then he picked up his bass, walked over, and knocked on the bus door.

I was astounded. The nerve! Pump a guy for details on how to take his job?

I had to remind myself I had never had a job someone else wanted. When I think back on it, the boys in the band were more compassionate than I gave them credit for. They assured me people did this all the time, and that if I wasn't doing a good enough job Monroe would surely let me know. In any case, he wasn't going to fire me after just a few weeks.

Still, it wore on me. Bill had made no promise—"We'll just see" was his degree of commitment.

The next day, on the long ride home, I was in the front of the bus sitting across from Bill, who was noodling around on the mandolin. I was reading a book, trying to be nonchalant about sitting there listening to Bill Monroe live in his living room, playing that famous Gibson F-5 Lloyd Loar mandolin with the gouged-out trademark on the headstock. He was doing some interesting things, pushing the edges of familiar tonality, working further and further outside, and then playing an odd, ascending arpeggio that ended in some crazy chord. I looked up from my book, surprised. He raised his eyebrows, satisfied he had gotten my attention. Then he went back to playing.

Having made this fleeting connection, I decided to pop the question. "So I was, uh, wondering if you thought I was doing good enough and, uh, whether I should, uh, bring my car down here and start looking around for a place to live."

His eyes narrowed a little, and he nodded just once, just barely.

It wasn't the affirmation I had hoped for, but it would have to do. Now I could go back to Milwaukee and get my car. Whether I would make enough money to avoid sleeping in it remained to be seen.

8 LEARNING THE VERNACULAR

(mainly archival)
About the only time we ever rehearsed was backstage at the Opry. Sometimes Bill would come in with an idea to do a tune he hadn't done in a while—perhaps one I'd never played with him—and we'd run it in the dressing room.

But the trickiest thing about playing the Opry might have been finding out ahead of time which suit we'd be wearing. Once, I had Bill on the phone, and he asked "How are the grays?" "Well, mine's kind of funky," I said, needing a trip to the dry cleaner's.

Later, in the dressing room, Bill said, "I heard somebody say their suit was *funnnky*. I ain't never heard that word around bluegrass."

This sort of thing happened all the time with Bill and me. As strange as he might have sounded to me, I'm sure I sounded stranger to him. "Uh, what is that?" he might ask. Or he might misunderstand me and get mad, thinking I was trying to show him up.

When we played in Boise, somehow everyone but me wound up with a souvenir lapel pin, a little plastic potato labeled *Idaho* in gold letters. When I was introduced I stepped forward and said, "Yes, I have no potato," and held out my taterless lapel. "I have no spud."

(During intermission someone stepped out of the audience and gave me one. Thanks, Boise!)

Monroe said "I ain't never heard o' nothin' called a spud. Back in Tennessee we call them Irish tomatoes."

So, *spud* is weird?

Esto Perpetua is the Idaho state motto. "Let it be perpetual."

One of my main problems in holding my own as Bill and the Boys razzed me was being able to understand what they were saying. Hillbilly jive can be like carny talk, unintelligible to the uninitiated.

A YANKEE DEVIL'S DICTIONARY (MINUS MANY IDIOMS)

airish: chilly

all: oil

all y'all: plural of y'all

an' 'em: and them, as in "Mama an' 'em"

are: hour

bait: bunch, group, as in "a big bait of beans"

bedclothes: sheets

bless his heart: dumbass

bluejohn: 2 percent or skim milk

blue meat: dark meat on a chicken or turkey

britches: breeches, or pants

can ye not: can't you

carry: accompany or convey, as in "Can I carry you home?"

close: hot and humid

cut the light off/on: turn the light off/on

dinner: lunch

directly: soon

doah: door

Do what?: "Beg your pardon."

'em 'r: them are

favors: looks like, resembles, as in "I believe he favors his father."

fern: foreign

fit to: suitable

fittin' to: getting ready to do something

fixin' to: getting ready to do something

flar: flower, flour

foundered: stuffed, fully surfeited

galluses: suspenders

gang up: gather

gitchy: get you, have, as in "Gitchy some more."

grip: suitcase

Hiyonchaygs?: "How do you want your eggs?"

holler: hollow

holler: yell

How're ye farin'?: "How are you faring/doing?"

I declare!: exclamation, "How about that?"

I never!: exclamation of disbelief

I swear!: see *I declare, I never*

'ja?: Did you?

kilver: cover

kindly: kind of, similar to

learn: teach

leave off: stop, quit

lick: attempt, as in "Hit it another lick"

liken unto: the same as, similar

like to: almost

likkity split: rapidly

mash: moonshine

mash: to push, press, exert pressure

maters: tomatoes

meat 'n three: southern restaurant entrée featuring chicken or meat and three sides

might: a little, as in "It's a might airish of a morning."

might could: might, could

might oughta: might, ought to

nary: narrow

nary: none, nil

nigh unto: near, nearly, close to

no 'count: no account, a ne'er-do-well

off'n: off of

okry: okra

parful: powerful; used as an intensifier, as in *parful lonesome*

poke: sack or bag

poke, poke salad: a poisonous weed made edible by prolonged boiling; greens

puts (me) in the mind of: reminds (me) of

put up: put away

raisin': upbringing

rare: rear, as in rear back

rarin': ready, eager

reckon: think, believe

rottenin': rotting

sorry: see *no 'count*

spell: a short period of time, or to relieve someone, as in "I'll spell you on guitar."

stove up: injured, sore

tags: license plates

tall cotton: excellent company

tar: tear

taters: potatoes

tetch: touch, slightly, a small amount

therebouts: near or around

they's: they are, they were, their

throwed: threw

throwed up his hand: waved

tote: bag

tote: carry

vittles: food or a meal, from victuals

wadn't: wasn't

weren't: wasn't

whale: whack or strike forcefully

whistlepig: groundhog

worry: annoy, irritate

y'all: you all, you, everybody

you'ns: variant of y'all

young'ns: children

Contributors: Janet Batrouny, Diane Bouska, Lee Cadillac, Nancy Cardwell Webster, T. Michael Coleman, Jeff Doggett, Tami Earley, P. T. Gazell, Doug Green, Ita Hardesty Mason, Dave Hollender, Becky Johnson, Richard Johnston, John Keith, Paul Kingsbury, Marty Lanham, Charlie Lowman, Beth Mattson-Hinzelin, Cindy Miller Bagwell, Steve Miller, James Price, Diane Shebilske, Chris Skinker, Richard Slayton, Danny Smith, Mary Ann Smith.

THE CRUCIBLE OF CHATOM 9

(recollected)

Moving to the South and joining Monroe's band was a deep dive into severe culture shock. When I spoke, people didn't understand me. Worse yet, I couldn't understand them. When I bought a pack of cigarettes and headed for the door, the clerk would call after me, "Come back," and I would turn around and come back in to see what he wanted. When I would call home, collect, it took several tries to give the operator my name.

"Mert?"

"Mark."

"Merk?"

And finally I would say, "Mork!"

"Ah-oh, *Mark!*"

This problem was compounded when the band was giving me shit, which was pretty much all the time. I couldn't understand half of it, and I didn't get many of the references, either. At any rate, I was in no position to rebut. And if I thought anything I had done musically before counted, I had to drop that notion.

I've never wanted to quit anything (though there have been instances when it would have been better if I had). But I came close to giving up a few times in those first few weeks in the band. One such time was my first visit to LA—Lower Alabama.

It was a festival at Lockwood Park, deep in the piney woods ten miles off Alabama State Route 17 south of Chatom, Alabama, in Washington County, about fifty miles north of Mobile, at the end of a dirt/sand road. The fine, powdery soil is easily stirred and coats everything—clothes, eyes, nasal passages, everything—with a thin layer of red dust as you go fishtailing through a bleak swampland full of rattlesnakes, copperheads, cottonmouths, and myriad other unfriendly creatures.

This was my first trip through the Deep South. My state of shock was about to turn progressive—stage 2—due to intolerance (my own). I was still getting used to being a hired hand, rather than a band member, and I suffered razzing and ridicule from the rest of the Boys, the bus driver, even old-timers among the fans. There are a lot of country folks who do like to kick a man when he's down.

As the bus rolled farther south, the scenery and the towns reminded me of footage I had seen of civil rights marches, the Freedom Riders, and movies like *In the Heat of the Night* and *Cool Hand Luke*.

Monroe saw I was a stranger in a strange land. As we crossed a long bridge at Demopolis, Alabama, he looked at me and said, "Boy, you are leavin' the country now!"

As barren as the festival park was, there wasn't much more around the motel where we stayed in Jackson. The only decent meal available was breakfast. There was a fly-infested chicken stand nearby that for all I knew might have been OK, but the looks of it quelled my appetite.

And the festival lasted a long four days. I guess Bill and the boys had a lot of friends around the park, so we didn't stay around the motel long before heading out there. Not that it was any more entertaining at the motel, but at least it was air conditioned. I don't think I've ever been any hotter than

I was there in August. I made a little small talk with strangers around the record table, but mostly it was a drawn-out ordeal of minding the records and fanning myself in that putrid heat.

Jim and Jesse McReynolds took pity on me one evening and invited me to join them for sandwiches with some friends who had an air-conditioned camping trailer. What a pleasant respite! They told me about days when they would play drive-in movie theaters around the South. Often, you'd need a ladder to get on the roof of the projector house. The mikes were wired to the drive-in's sound system, so people in their cars would hear the music on those little speakers you hung on your window for the movie. When the song was through, they'd honk their horns, and if they really liked it they might flash their lights. Laughing about it, Jim and Jesse said they never got used to that.

That was easily the high point of the four days. On the last day, one of the food stands was serving red beans and rice, the best meal I had that weekend. Another food stand was run by a local civic group called the Quarterback Club. I heard a rumor—perhaps fabricated for my Yankee benefit—that it was a front for the KKK. That was easy to believe.

At long last our evening spot came up, the final set of the festival. But before we could go, the owner of the land wanted to offer a few words.

In his white shirt and overalls, he really looked like a denizen of Dixie, a character right out of *To Kill a Mockingbird*. His voice boomed out over the audience.

"Ah shuah hope y'all have enjawed the show," he said. "Ah hope it wadn't too loud for ye. We don't 'llow no niggah jumpin' music 'round heah!" he said, drawing laughter and some applause.

Then, Monroe, as he often did when we were closing out a festival, called on each of the Blue Grass Boys to say a few words. My turn came last.

"And back here on the bass, from the state of Wisconsin, this is little Markie Hembree. Little Markie, would you like to say a few words to these nice people?"

More laughter. Maybe it was the heat, or the lack of a decent meal in days, or the revulsion and alienation, but I had had it. I didn't care if I lost my job.

"Well sure, *Billy*," I said, and gave him a sidelong look. And paused.

Now, one did not ever call Monroe *Billy*, especially in front of a crowd of redneck fans. There was a stunned silence and a little nervous giggling (probably the women thinking, "Oh, bless his heart!").

Monroe glared back at me and said nothing. Then Wayne, off-mike but loud enough to be heard, said, "Boss, you want me to kill him now or later?"

The crowd cracked up, then applauded. I was pretty sure if they hadn't laughed I'd have been fired. But I didn't care.

I have heard others say that Monroe would push you until he found your limit. And Ricky Skaggs stated a corollary, that Monroe wouldn't really respect you unless you got up in his face. So, as it worked out, things got a little easier for me after that. I had to pick my moments, but being a wise guy and standing my ground actually helped.

10 COMFORT LEVEL 1

(recollected)

I bought a Chevy Vega for $325 in Milwaukee in the winter of 1978. My future father-in-law, a plant boss at Harnischfeger, knew a guy named Miguel who fixed cars and ran a little business out of his garage in Milwaukee's Riverwest neighborhood. A foot switch on the floor, like an old-time headlight dimmer, served as a starter button; you pressed it down and turned the key.

When the car began running rough a couple of days later, I brought it back, indignant. Miguel was annoyed. He started it up, raised the hood, and gave the distributor cap a half turn, and it began idling smoothly. The look he gave me said, "You little gringo, what do you expect for $325?"

When I joined Bill in July 1979, I left the car in Milwaukee, not sure whether I actually had a job or whether the car would be able to make the five-hundred-mile trip. Weighing a week's lodging against airfare and my desire to see Georgia—she still hadn't decided whether she was going to move to Nashville—I often flew back to Milwaukee between gigs.

So, in August I decided to see whether the Vega would make the trip. It ran hot, so I turned the heater on full blast to keep the radiator from boiling over and drove all day through the midsummer swelter of Indiana. By sunset I was south of Indianapolis, and as the cool of evening came on I began to believe I would actually make it.

When I arrived at the Astro Motel on Dickerson Pike that night, I was jubilant. I had made it! I had a car! Unimpressed, the manager checked me in.

Somehow this car seemed to bring me luck, though driving around Nashville in August with the heater running was pretty unpleasant. (A couple of years later, Blake countered my boast that it always started in cold weather, saying, "It ought to. Them pistons ain't touchin' nothin'.")

On off days I went cruising around town in my four-wheeled sauna, looking for a place to rent. One afternoon I took a break and stopped at a Wendy's to drink a soda and get some air conditioning. I must have looked pretty miserable, because a waitress offered me an additional cup of ice water. I took a long drink, thanked her, and asked her dejectedly whether she knew of any place for rent.

Actually, she did. She was moving out of her apartment in East Nashville and didn't think the landlady had another renter yet. And it was cheap, forty dollars a week.

So I took a drive down Riverside Drive, found the place, and rented a two-room upper. Things were looking up. And I still had my job.

A GENTLE SIDE OF BILL 11

(archival)

It was a short ride up to Somerset, Kentucky, from Nashville on a beautiful autumn evening, golden sunlight dazzling the fields as rows of crops spun past.

We were playing a high school that night. When we arrived, two local fellows, possibly maintenance workers at the school, were there to greet the bus, running around excitedly and waving in six different directions, trying to show us where to park.

Both of them seemed intellectually disabled—what some country folk might call "slow" or "simple." When I stepped out to unload the record concessions, one of them trotted up, eager to help, all smiles, so excited to see the bus and meet Bill. I thanked him and said there's not much to it, maybe you can carry a box for me.

I opened one of the cargo bay doors and began to lift it. He jumped to it, pushing the door farther up. "Whoa whoa whoa!" I yelled, trying to stop him from pushing it too far and breaking the hinge. I handed him a box of records, and he took off with it, running toward the building.

Once inside the gym where we would play, I had more such help as we waltzed around with two long, heavy tables. I was trying to direct my helpers to a certain spot, rather than all of us wandering around the basketball court with these things.

Once we had settled the concessions, I wanted to retreat to the locker room, our dressing room, to get away. But one of my helpers wanted to know whether he could meet Bill, Mr. Bill, Mr. Bill Monroe from the Grand Ole Opry. I was hesitant to bother Monroe, but this guy just had to meet him. "Let's see if he's come in yet," I said, and we went to the locker room.

Monroe was there, and this fellow was so excited that he ran over and picked up the mandolin case and held it out to him, asking if he would play it.

Bill's response disarmed me. He gently took the case back and laid it on a bench, then told the young man to sit right there and listen. The guy sat down, slapping his knees, and Bill calmed him a little, then took out the mandolin, threw the strap over his shoulder, and began to play, looking him in the eye and swaying a little to the music, swooping and bobbing with the riffs, occasionally holding up a hand to hush him. Gradually, the guy relaxed and sat listening, rapt.

I felt small for having been irritated. But more than that, I admired a compassionate side of Bill I had never seen. It was a pure act of kindness— not for someone he wanted to impress, not even for anyone he knew. Just for that one fellow.

Perhaps it was because he knew what it was like to have a disability or to be thought "slow," like that little cross-eyed boy back in Rosine who ran and hid from strangers.

(recollected)

Located in Indiana's Brown County, Bean Blossom is about a half hour from Bloomington and an hour south of Indianapolis. But it became central to my personal experience of "real" bluegrass music.

Sure, there was country music in Wisconsin where I grew up, about six hours to the north. There was even bluegrass, which I probably wouldn't have known much about if not for my dad.

But it wasn't the same as hearing the first-generation masters who performed at Bill Monroe's festival. Lester Flatt, Jimmy Martin, Don Reno and Bill Harrell, Jim & Jesse, the Osborne Brothers, Ralph Stanley, Del McCoury, J. D. Crowe, Carl Story—you could see all of them and many more in a single day at Bean Blossom.

The eighty-acre lot was home to the Brown County Jamboree, a Sunday night country music show that had been going on since 1941. It started as an impromptu roadside attraction and became so popular the owners built a barnlike music hall for it. Monroe first played there in 1951 and bought the place the next year. The Jamboree continued every Sunday night, May to November. Bill played there often, and even when he wasn't performing he was enjoying the rest of the wooded land, fox hunting or just running his dogs.

With the advent of folk music festivals, Monroe decided to try his own hand at putting on a show there. But, perhaps to distance himself from the Yankee folkies, he avoided calling it a "festival." His 1967 event was called a "Blue Grass Music Celebration." In 1968, it drew ten thousand people. By the mid-1970s, the crowds had grown to thirty-five thousand, then fifty thousand.

The setting was rustic, and, especially in the early days, the facilities were disastrously inadequate. Shure Vocal Master PA speakers lashed to trees provided clipped, distorted sound. Before porta potties, the privies were unspeakable. The music barn, out at the front of the park, was little more than a ramshackle, leaky roof held up by clapboards. By the time I first saw it, it was merely the rainy day alternate venue.

But the park was perfect for a festival. Unlike the featureless, flat fields that make a drive through Indiana on I-65 so monotonous, Brown County is hilly and lush. When you entered the festival grounds from Highway 135, you took a gravel road past the music barn through a big open field (mostly dedicated to parking but dotted with campers and tents) to a stand of tall, slender trees that sheltered a natural amphitheater. If you continued in the same direction, there was another open field for camping. At the bottom of the theater bowl, behind the stage, was a pond where bullfrogs held loud late-night jam sessions. A gravel drive went past to another campground, surrounded by trees, on the other side of the pond. In the opposite direction was another large field filled with campers and motor homes, and more trees and camping beyond. This was the Amen Corner, where sometimes well-known players were afforded some anonymity for late-night postshow activities, jamming and whatnot.

At first glance, the trees that stood throughout the audience area would be seen as obstructions. But once you were used to it, the view wasn't that bad. And the shade the canopy of leaves afforded was most welcome on a hot, sunny day in Southern Indiana. The "seats" were benches made of long planks atop short stumps. But if you were careful about splinters, those weren't bad, either.

At the top of the amphitheater, behind the audience, were three little whitewashed shacks. The smallest was Bill's concession stand, where I spent many hours minding the store. Another was a first-aid station. And the third was Birch Monroe's "refreshment" stand, where Bill's brother sold tiny hamburgers, hot dogs, coffee, and soda.

There never was a better venue for an outdoor festival. In the late afternoon, the sun slanted through the trees and gave the day's dust an iridescence that made the place look like an impressionist painting. At night, a merciful coolness swept through the audience, and the dew settled the dust of the day as the stars came out.

Right after high school graduation in 1974, having recently converted from Crosby, Stills & Nash to Monroe, Flatt & Scruggs, I grabbed a girl and hitchhiked to Bean Blossom. Neither her parents nor mine were pleased when they found out. Dad drove down from Wisconsin to fetch us—but not before taking in the day's show.

Five years later, Mom and Dad came to Bean Blossom for the autumn festival and their first time of seeing me perform with Monroe. Mom was always more a fan of Mozart than of Monroe, but now she seemed less disdainful of my career choice. At least I was wearing a suit. When I asked her what she thought of the show, she said it was pretty good, but Dad was going to need some help. Every button he had was busted.

UNCLE BIRCH 13

(recollected)

Whatever hardships Bill endured at the hands of his older brothers while he was growing up were not forgotten.

Peter Rowan told me a story about driving Monroe around on the north side of Nashville when he pointed at a driveway and told Peter to pull in. Peter drove up, and Bill got out and walked to the house. A man answered the door, and Bill decked him with a single punch. Then he returned to the car and told Peter to go.

They rode along in silence for a minute or two until Peter finally asked who that was. "That was Charlie," Bill said.

"Charlie?"

"My brother," Bill said, and offered no further explanation.

Even when Monroe was in his seventies, it seemed he was still paying them back. Bill's brother Birch Monroe, known to the fans at Bean Blossom as Uncle Birch, stoically endured almost daily abuse. Rail-thin, frail, and soft-spoken, Birch mostly just nodded when Bill was directing him or taking him to task for something.

Birch managed the property at Bean Blossom and lived nearby. It was his duty to maintain the grounds there and at the Monroe Music Land Park in Beaver Dam, Kentucky, about ten miles from Rosine, where he and Bill grew up.

And maintain them Birch did—both places always looked like they were about to fall down. The facilities were beyond rustic. It was a wonder to watch him at work, whether it was testing a "repaired" door hanging at an angle from a shiny new set of hinges or telling the help to use less grounds in the coffee (which already tasted like hot water in a used cup).

At Bean Blossom, with tens of thousands of captive customers, Birch's little refreshment shack did a booming business. The burgers were tiny, and usually in short supply. Birch would send someone down to the IGA to buy ground beef, one or two pounds at a time, along with another dozen buns.

To call Birch miserly would be inadequate. Buck White told me about a time, perhaps in the 1960s, when he went up to Indiana to help reroof the music barn. When he got there, he found they had everything they needed except, unaccountably, roofing nails. He told Birch everything looked fine but they were going to need nails.

The closest hardware store was probably in Morgantown or Martinsville, ten or twenty miles away, so Birch was gone awhile. He returned with a one-dollar bag of nails.

At Bean Blossom, Wayne, Butch, and I were assigned to back Birch daily for two thirty-minute sets of old-time fiddle tunes. "Carroll County Blues" and "Coming Down from Boston" were his big hits, delivered in doddering style. We were never paid anything extra for these two sets a day for the ten days of the festival. Nor were we afforded a break at the concession stand—we paid full price for every cup of almost-coffee.

One year I was asked at the last minute to host the band contest. I sent a kid up the hill to Birch's stand to get the day's program, and told him to tell Birch I had sent him. The kid came back with a program and said I owed him $1.25.

14 "DOGHOUSE BLUES"

(archival)

People ask what happens when Monroe gets mad. The answer—nothing. And if he's really angry, nothing happens for a really long time.

Three months later this story bears telling. Last June, the day before the Bean Blossom festival, Bill asked whether I'd drive a truck there from Tennessee. Wayne jumped in and said, "Aw, it's not hard. It's just that old cattle truck. It's only got ten forward gears."

Well, I thought then they were pulling my leg.

I wasn't crazy about going up a day early, and when I saw the opportunity to ride up there with Wayne and Butch, I went to Monroe and told him that's what I'd like to do.

Bill was pissed. "Ain't you gonna help me?"

"Boss, you know I can't drive that cattle truck," I said.

"Why, it ain't no cattle truck, it's my pickup!"

"Oh, well, hell, Boss, I can drive that alright if you want."

"No, I asked you once and you said no, so let's just leave it there. I never ask a man for a favor twice. I never will forget this!"

And he hasn't. Nor has he spoken to me in the past three months.

PROPER GROOMING AND A TIP OF THE HAT 15

(recollected)

A Blue Grass Boy's uniform starts with the shoes. Southern folks judge a man by his shoes. Even in casual dress, shoes are held to a higher standard than up north.

My father, a North Carolinian, held this view. He grew up during the Great Depression: his sisters wore dresses made from feed sacks, and all the kids went barefoot until school started and they got a pair of shoes for the year.

So, every fall Dad would march all five of us kids down to Heckert's to buy the biggest, ugliest shoes possible. No penny loafers. No Hush Puppies or anything trendy. My sisters would cry and wail, but Dad would insist and Mom would back him up. Arms out, palms up, she would say, "This is up to your father."

Nevertheless, in my generation, shoe polishing was a dying art. So I was glad to have this skill in my background. Further discussions with the Boys refined my techniques—what kind of polish to use, how much, how to apply it. Too much will build up and crack. A good shine kit needs a toothbrush to work the soles. Do it right, and you can get by with buffing alone for the next two or three times. If I fell behind, Bill would look down at my shoes, then up at me for an explanation. Yeah, I got in a hurry and forgot to buff 'em, I might say. I'd make sure they were polished the next time he saw them.

The trickiest thing about the suits was choosing dry-cleaning cycles wisely. You didn't want to get caught without whatever suit Bill chose for a show. If you could catch Bill's secretary at her desk on a Friday, she would know what we'd be wearing on the Opry Friday and Saturday. Otherwise, it might take several more calls to find out.

Ties came with the suits. Butch showed me how to use a straight razor to lightly scrape the pills off the polyester and keep the tie looking sharp.

Shirts were easy—white, short-sleeve ("shirt sleeves," as they say in the South), worn with or without coats. That's why Dad went out and bought me six of them (along with a pair of big, ugly black dress shoes) when I got the job.

Ah, but the hat! A Blue Grass Boy is not properly dressed without one. The band wore straw hats in the summer, then switched to Stetsons in the fall. I found a suitable straw hat, but I wasn't ready for the change of seasons.

Nowadays, a Stetson can run $200–$300. In 1979, you could get one for $60–$75. But the year I started with Monroe, he was paying $50 per day—and that was only on the days you worked. So, you could leave Nashville on a Thursday night, play in New York on a Friday night and Boston on Saturday, and come home perhaps late Sunday night or early Monday morning with $100 for your week's pay, minus meals.

On one such trip near the end of September, we were on the way home and Bill was telling us about the work we had coming up, including a trip to the White House and a presidential concert at Ford's Theatre.

Baker said, "We'd better go to the felts, hadn't we?"

Bill nodded. "Reckon so."

I had to ask. Felts? What do you mean felts?

Felt hats, Wayne explained. We wear straws in the summer, and then we switch to the felts for winter. He told me the different brands and where I could shop for them. Stetson was the most expensive, but there were others that were a little less, maybe a Resistol or a Beaver.

I nodded as if I understood, but he could probably see my wheels turning. The low pay and trips back to Milwaukee had left me stretched thin. I had maybe $120 in my pocket for the week, and I needed to spend $60 or $70 on a hat. It might as well have been $200, because I didn't have it. Unless I skipped the hat, I wouldn't be able to eat and pay rent.

The absurdity of it drove me to tears. I was playing with a Grand Ole Opry star, the Father of Blue Grass no less, and I couldn't buy a hat without going homeless. Here I was sweating bullets over a damned cowboy hat.

I almost quit. Instead, I called Dad and he wired me $50. And I found a Beaver for $35.

A month later, I was a guest of President Carter, lunching at the White House and dining at the Watergate, all expenses paid.

Good thing I had a nice hat.

PART III
"BREAKING IN A BRAND-NEW PAIR OF SHOES"

(recollected)

In October 1979, *A Celebration of Country Music* was the first country music concert in the history of Ford's Theatre in Washington, DC. With guests invited by President Jimmy Carter and paying $250 a ticket, it was a fundraiser for the theater's renovation. Starring Dolly Parton, Eddie Rabbitt, Barbara Mandrell, Loretta Lynn, the Oak Ridge Boys, Larry Gatlin, Dottie West, Johnny Cash, Freddy Fender, Glen Campbell, the Statler Brothers, Tom T. Hall, Ray Stevens, Charlie Rich, Lynn Anderson, and Bill Monroe, the show was taped live and broadcast in prime time on NBC.

At last I could honestly say I had made the big time, if only for a few hours to go along for the ride.

Shortly after arriving at the Watergate Hotel and paying room service $15 for a sandwich and a beer, I learned Uncle Sam was covering the tab. It would have been nice if someone had told me about that ahead of time. But those sorts of details were always hard to come by in Monroe's band.

Now that I knew, I decided to spread the wealth. I called an old bandmate in Maryland and invited him and his partner for dinner. I could hear her in the background: "The Watergate? I can't go to the Watergate!" Tell her not to worry, I said. Come as you are. We'll dine in.

Room service delivered our dinner and a bottle of wine to the balcony, and we had a grand time. I signed the bill with a generous tip. It came to about $300, a rebate on the self-employment tax I had been paying as a musician for the previous five years.

In the couple of days in DC before the concert, we were shuttled around town in limousines to events that had been planned for the show's cast. There was a reception at the Corcoran Gallery of Art, where Speaker of the House Tip O'Neill (D-MA) presided and lived up to his nickname. When the music cranked up, it was big-band swing. I asked a glamorous young woman to dance, and she accepted, but Larry Gatlin cut in midway through. The Boys got a kick out of that. "Looks like you're out of your league," Monroe said. "You done been shot out of the saddle," Baker added.

And there was a party at the home of Senate minority leader Howard Baker (R-TN). We made our way into the house through a phalanx of press with video cameras, lights, and long-range microphones they held out to us as we passed. "By god, you know what that is, don't you?" Baker said. "They're checkin' for gats, that's what."

The day of the show, the whole cast attended a luncheon at the White House. Standing in line to enter the East Room, each of us posed for a photo with the president and first lady. The Blue Grass Boys were near the front of this line, with the more-famous coming later in the queue. Left on our own in the East Room, we wandered around and wondered where to sit.

There were no place cards other than one for the president, at a table next to the fireplace. "We could sit here, couldn't we?" Monroe said. I said I thought it might be best to wait for an invitation. But what would I know? Bill and the band began to seat themselves, and I reluctantly pulled out a chair. As I was lowering myself into it—I was actually on my way down—Ronnie Milsap's manager threw himself under me and said, "I really wanted to sit here. Do you mind?"

So, I sat at the next table with Johnny Cash and Dottie West. They talked about their families, the origin of their names, and forebears—"Of course, there's a lot of trash in there, too," Cash allowed—as well as mansion security systems.

Asked later about what he had discussed with the president, Monroe said they talked about peanut farming. Butch and I wondered whether Carter even knew who Monroe was. Carter probably would have preferred lunching with Dolly Parton.

The invitation had called for black tie, which drew several interpretations from the country musicians. Predictably, Cash wore his usual black suit with long coat. Freddy Fender wore a white tux and a frilly shirt with fine black piping, looking as if he had come straight from a Mexican wedding gig.

Weeks before, when we received our invitations, I had unsuccessfully tried to point out that "black tie" meant tuxedos. Instead, Monroe ordered up some Taiwanese shiny polyester, three-piece black suits and black ties.

Anyway, the filet mignon, served on the Johnson china, was excellent. I learned about the plates from a society column in the *Washington Post*. The same column reported that our band, in our black suits, looked like a morticians' convention.

At Ford's Theatre for the dress rehearsal, I was wandering around killing time and waiting our turn when Dolly Parton came out to run through her number. I sat out in the house, front and center, while she sang *I Will Always Love You* to me. The whole song. To me.

When she had finished, I slumped in my seat and gave a low whistle and tugged at my collar to let the steam escape. She giggled and chirped, "You're sweet!"

"Oh, Miss Dolly!" I called back, holding up my hands in surrender.

When our turn came, Bill worried that he wouldn't be able to sing. He had a bad cold and cough, and it was getting worse. We ran "Blue Moon of Kentucky," Bill almost whispering the waltz section and holding back on the up-tempo part that followed. He was hoping he had just one good one in him that day.

And he did. During the live taping, with the president sitting in the front row, Monroe worked cautiously through the waltz portion, taking advantage of the mike level that had been set during rehearsal. But when the band sprang into two-four time, he leaned into that red-hot mike and bore down hard, blowing away the first few rows. I saw Carter's eyes bug out, and it definitely shook up the audience.

Dolly had introduced us, and now she waited to walk us off. Being last in line with my bass, I offered her my arm; she took it with both hands and whispered in my ear, "Y'all are so good!" "Was it alright?" I asked. "If it was any better I couldn't have stood it!" she said.

The next morning the *Washington Post* agreed. The review generally panned the show as a tired display of commercialized country music, with the exception of Bill Monroe and the Blue Grass Boys, who "electrified" the audience.

As I read the paper, the phone rang. It was Monroe. "Did you see the newspaper?" he asked. He was pumped. "Yes, sir," I said, "I sure did."

"Now be dressed when you come downstairs, hear?" he said. He wanted the Boys looking their best when they hit the lobby.

So I was decked out in my suit when room service arrived with breakfast. I marveled at my good fortune. Here I was, high on a balcony at the Watergate, eating breakfast off a silver service, watching helicopters plying the Potomac below, having coffee and a post-breakfast cigar and savoring our rave review in the *Washington Post*. The big time! This would be so easy to get used to.

We were chauffeured in a limousine to the airport for our flight to Los Angeles. As we approached the boarding gate, we encountered members of the NBC production crew heading home.

When they saw Bill, they cracked up. "Look out! Here comes Mr. Blue Moon!" One of them told us he was in the sound truck parked in the alley behind Ford's Theatre, and when Bill hit that hot mike full-on they threw off their headphones. "Buddy, that wasn't no silver moon, weren't no harvest moon, that wasn't nothin' but a *ba-LUE* moon!"

But when we arrived in Los Angeles that evening, the airline had lost our luggage. Bill thought we should stay close to the airport until they brought our bags. So, we checked into a run-down motel near LAX called the Little Sands. The beds were misshapen, and there were holes in the towels.

Less than twelve hours separated us from our accommodations at the Watergate. *Sic transit gloria mundi*: thus passes worldly glory, I reckon.

17 THE EYE

(archival)

As intense as the music he plays is the fearsome gaze Monroe can fix on someone who displeases him. Not just any baleful glare or icy stare—it's more like a searing, psychic laser. Former band members still shudder and laugh when you mention getting The Eye.

He could burn a hole in your forehead with a sidelong glance. You'd see just a sliver of his eye, but that was enough. The same personal force that enabled him to captivate a stadium audience was devastating at close range.

My favorite example is when we checked in at the Watergate. We had come from Columbus, Ohio, where all the Blue Grass Boys were given baby blue windbreakers with "Bluegrass Palace, Columbus, Ohio" spelled out in firelog letters on the back. Great at a festival or a ballgame. Hardly *de rigueur* at the Watergate.

But it was a rainy, blustery day when we landed in DC, so all of us put on the jackets (except Bill, who wore a navy blue pinstripe suit and overcoat). Wearing western hats and satin windbreakers with hillbilly script on the back, we were making a country music fashion statement in a swanky setting.

Still, we were in Washington at the invitation of the president for a concert at Ford's Theatre, and Uncle Sam was footing the bill. As the paperwork was completed—everything prepaid—the desk clerk, thinking he was being witty, sneered, "Will this be check or cash?"

Monroe didn't look angry, or amused, or anything else. He squared himself and simply *looked* at the guy, silently, and a hush fell over the desk. The clerk mumbled, "Yes, sir," pushed the keys across the counter, and got himself the hell away from there.

We laughed all the way to the rooms. I guess any Blue Grass Boy likes to watch The Eye work on someone else. Anyone else. Please.

MORE ON THE BUS 18

(archival)

The first national touring I did was with the Monroe Doctrine in a Ford Econoline van. We were based in Denver, but most of our work was in the Midwest or on the East Coast—grueling trips. Logging thousand-mile rides on a bench seat was tough, and the van wasn't getting any younger, either. Its last trip, from Milwaukee to Denver, took about seventy-two hours because it broke down seven times. We upgraded to a Wayne Busette, a Chevy van conversion, and installed two pairs of bus seats behind the driver and shotgun seat, plus a raised deck over the cargo area with a padded top that could sleep two. That was luxurious.

But it was nothing like riding a Silver Eagle bus. Continental Trailways ran them, and they were nicer than a Greyhound. Monroe's bus was thirty-seven feet long, twelve and a half feet tall, and a big step up for me.

At first, anyway. Familiarity does breed contempt. How quickly we become accustomed to everyday life despite what every day used to be like before.

Like Monroe's office, the bus features shag carpeting and wood-burned plaques. There is a pattern of grime on the walls where the airflow from the AC unit strikes them. The carpeting has an acoustic dampening effect that cannot be discounted. But it is passing ugly. Further exploration may lead to the discovery of new life-forms.

And now that the novelty has worn off, I must admit the bus stinks. It smells of socks and drawers, pickled vegetables and rotted, potted meats, body odor, mouth odor, diesel fumes, hot rubber, and the variegated bouquet of the john, the door of which is an arm's length away from my bunk. The toilet is not a functional flusher, just a piss receptacle. It hasn't been cleaned out in Lord knows how long.

This is at the back of the bus, home of the Blue Grass Boys on the road. Four of us sleep in a six-by-seven-foot area over the Detroit diesel engine, which doubles as a smoke-screen generator (they'll never find us). On a long trip, the floor is warm to the touch as heat from the engine makes its way upward.

Aside from these considerations, the bus is mechanically deficient. The brakes are going bad—might have a loose shoe. The clutch is going bad. We have to work the door latch with a screwdriver to get off the bus.

Franz (the latest driver) has been slow to institute improvements. The john smell is awful, so Franz is ordered to drain and clean it; the AC is clogged with scum and doesn't work, so Monroe tells Franz to get after that, and so on.

My favorite so far is Bill not being able to do the screwdriver trick on the door. In his frustration, he broke the handle off the latch and would have missed the second set if Wayne hadn't sent someone back to the bus to check on him. He was there, alright, locked in.

So that repair was ordered, too. I just hope we don't have to roll off a mountain before the brakes and clutch are fixed.

19 ROAD CUISINE

(archival)

If you have trouble gaining weight you can go on the Bill Monroe regimen.

He liked being up at dawn. But keeping a farmer's schedule would have meant winding down after sunset, and, of course, as a headliner he closed most shows, so that was impossible.

On bus trips, the meal schedule was:

Breakfast: 6:30 A.M. (at the latest).

Lunch: 11:30 A.M. (this was the big meal, "meat and three" being the ideal. Usually this meant a pork chop or chicken with three sides, mostly vegetables, either fried or boiled into submission, southern style).

Supper: Could be around 6:00 P.M. or 7:00 P.M. on off days, but otherwise it would be after the show, maybe 10:00 or 11:00 at night. Then we'd get back on the bus and go to sleep. All those late meals started filling out my skinny frame.

Never being an early riser, I often missed breakfast, which is still easy to do down south. The best southern breakfast spots—that means biscuits, choice of red-eye or sausage gravy, cornbread, grits, and pancakes or toast, along with ham, bacon, or sausage to go with your eggs—slam it shut at 10:00 A.M. or 10:30 A.M.

Damn.

Because I like breakfast, especially a southern breakfast, I would try to drag myself out of the bunk at reveille. These forays in a semiconscious state produced dreamlike memories.

One morning, somewhere in Arizona, the bus was parked on the shoulder of a busy highway. Exiting on the right side of the bus, unaware of my surroundings, I walked around the front toward the restaurant across the road. As I stepped out from in front of the bus, an eighteen-wheeler roared past, missing me by a foot or two. I lunged backward, now wide awake.

Baker stood there, grinning. "Mark, don't walk in front of that truck. That thing might hurt you!"

Meal times were perhaps the chief source of my personal interactions with Monroe. We might converse on the bus or before a show, but not a lot. It was mostly over the table. It was a way to gauge his mood and whether you were OK with him (or not). There was a fine line between him poking fun at you and running you down. But, at any rate, it was when he was the most talkative.

Among his general observations:

"I love ham. You can't hurt ham," he famously said. On the country variety, dry and briny, I would agree. It is impervious.

Holding a cold, stale biscuit and motioning a throw: "*Man*, I could really curve one of these!"

Bill's avowed favorite food of all: fried potatoes. Later, after colon surgery: sweet-and-sour chicken.

Regarding my "dippin' eggs" (over easy, the way Dad cooked them for me): "That hen's worked hard to keep them two parts separate, and now you go running them all together."

Upon seeing me, trying to be polite, take knife and fork to a piece of chicken: "Down south here we just pick up the chicken and get after it like a dog on a bone." I decided not to tell him my mother always made us ask for permission to eat like Flintstones.

"Man, I love that Greek food!" But I think what he really liked was the six- or eight-page menu you could find at a Greek diner. He wouldn't go for the moussaka. But fried chicken? You bet.

And always dessert. He would sit back, raise his hands in supplication, and say, "We could have some pah, couldn't we?"

I don't think he cared much for Mexican fare, and I know he didn't like Indian food. In London, we thought we'd have better luck walking out to an Indian restaurant for supper, since Bill had complained about the food at the hotel being so "sorry." (By the way, "English cuisine" is a contradiction in terms.)

Monroe was game. But he didn't care for the beef dish we ordered for him. He looked up at the waiter, waving his hands, and asked whether they had any bread.

"Bread? Oh yes!" the waiter answered, and promptly returned with a basket of na'an. Bill picked up a piece and waved it like a fan. "Sht!" I thought for a moment he might flip it like a Frisbee.

It could have been worse. On our walk back to the hotel, Monroe, looking the wrong way on an English thoroughfare, stepped off the curb to cross. Butch and I yanked him back just as a taxi whizzed by his outstretched foot.

"I'm glad you boys is stout," Bill said, a bit shaken.

At times when he was annoyed with Monroe, Butch would express regret for that.

That night at supper, he and Bill had gotten into it about the live album (*Bean Blossom '79*). Butch said he had tapes he'd made himself that beat the album. The discussion went on, and at one point Butch leaned over the table, jabbed his finger at Monroe, and said, "You don't know it, but I can be just as hardheaded as you can."

Bill slammed both hands on the table and shot back, "Oh no you can't!"

(archival)

The night before, Bill didn't say what time he wanted to leave in the morning. Franz (the driver) comes to my room in the morning and tells me it's 10 a.m. (Faintly, to myself) "Awfuck."

Emerging instantly—as instantly as I can get dressed while half awake with less than two consecutive hours of sleep under my belt (my belt, where's my damn belt)—I bolt from the motel room. Squinting in the morning light, I see Granny Squirrel's Restaurant up the hill, and the cowboy-hatted silhouette of Monroe paying his check.

Awfuck. And then, awfuckit. In a sleep-addled decision, I decide to go get breakfast anyway, so I'm late getting on the bus. They're all waiting when I get on. Awfuck.

Monroe is pissed and threatens to start waking people up at seven, and that goes for all the Blue Grass Boys. "So damn it, be more prompt," says Baker.

And Monroe stays pissed. And when he plays against you, you can't play. I play like shit that night.

Now it's a six-hour ride back to Nashville. Mon's got nothing to say to me except when I joked about Wayne marking the cards when he beat Bill at gin. Says Butch and I ruined the cards.

Well, now *I'm* pissed. Because of a bad window gasket, the cards got soaked when we were in Portland, Oregon, and it was probably Monroe who played them while they were still wet. I am thinking to myself it damn sure wasn't me, and I get no thanks for the work I do for a pittance simply for the love of the music he has created and which I do my best to play when he isn't fucking with me onstage, and when he is, too.

"Well, no, that ain't my fault," I say.

"We ain't gonna wait on you no more," he says. "When it's time to go you be ready."

"It would help me a lot to know when we're going to leave," I say.

"You ought to be man enough to get out of bed of a morning," he says.

This is how it usually goes.

No key: At this writing we are in North Carolina for a week. The lock on the bus has been changed, and the driver has provided Bill with five keys in addition to his own. I still don't have one. How would you like it if you lived in a hotel but had to rely on a desk clerk who is only occasionally behind the desk to get into your room? This has gone on for two months now.

No itinerary: On a monthlong West Coast tour, we had no advance knowledge of our schedule. We had only rumors to go on until we reached Pocatello, Idaho, three days out. I still didn't know where we'd be the next day or for the rest of the month. When we pull into town to play, I have no idea where we're staying or even if we are staying.

No prep: Word is we'll be recording an album either this month or the next, and I'm still not sure he'll even use me on the album. If we're playing a show and someone requests a song that has three verses and a chorus of bass singing and I don't know the words, Bill says, "Well, do the best you can."

This is when you sing without consonants.

I am not the only one who suffers from this lack of communication. When I joined the band, Georgia wasn't sure she wanted to move to Tennessee at all. And for several weeks, I wasn't sure how long I would be living there. When she did move to Nashville, it was less than a year before I proposed to her. Funny, though—she and her mother insisted they wanted to know ahead of time when the wedding would be. We chose January, when the band's schedule would be sparse enough to bet on an open date.

Not quite sparse enough, though. I had to cut our honeymoon short because Monroe didn't bother to tell me we were going to Toronto to do a television show. (It was the *Tommy Hunter Show*, Canada's cross between the *Tonight Show* and a country music showcase; *Hee Haw* with fewer hay bales.)

Not that he runs the band for my benefit, but these things would be nice to know. I flew from Milwaukee to Nashville in time to fly to Toronto.

When the band flew, a bass would be provided at the venue. This was always chancy, and in Toronto, when a man came to the studio's green room carrying a bass in a cheap-looking Naugahyde cover, I was apprehensive. The man assured me they (people at the music store?) had provided the best instrument they had. Pulling the cover off revealed what looked like a junior-high student bass. And it was missing a string.

The Boys and I were still laughing when Bill walked into the room. "Boss, they really lined up a good one this time," I said.

"What's the matter with it?" he asked, looking annoyed.

"Well, it's only got three strings," I said.

"Which one's missing?"

"The E string," I said, showing him, "the low one."

"You don't need that one nohow," he concluded.

True enough. If I had to give one up, that would be the one; I could work around it. Still, I didn't like going on national TV with a three-string bass.

THE BEER TABOO 21

(archival)

As far as Bill is concerned, liquor is OK in moderation—it is a man's drink with a man's taste. "Why, I love the taste of whiskey," he says. Actually, he's pretty much a teetotaler who will nurse a half glass of wine all night.

Beer—"that old slop"—is *not* OK, not in any amount. "There is nothing as sloppy as a big old glass of beer just a'sittin' there with that foam on it," he'd say. Telling about his older brothers, he said, "They'd come in from them beer joints, and their shirts, their breath, would smell of it." I suspect that was his association: his older brothers coming in late, sloppy drunk, probably waking him up to mess with him.

Butch had a different theory: "If horses didn't piss on flat rocks you wouldn't have this problem."

It didn't matter which of the boys, where, or when, Bill had beer radar. At Bean Blossom, Baker could be off in a far part of the grounds, standing behind a tree, crack open a can, look up, and there would be Monroe. It never failed.

On a flight to Hawai'i, I sat far forward of Monroe, conversing with a uniformed US Air Force officer, who bought me a beer. Later, I wanted to return the favor. I stepped into the aisle, looked aft in the cabin, and saw Monroe asleep, his head back, mouth agape. I walked past him to the galley, paid the flight attendant for two beers, turned around, and there Bill stood, blocking my way.

"Why you got to drink 'em two at a time?" he demanded. I told him the other was for the air force fella I was sitting with. "Sht! I don't see why you got to drink that ol' slop."

It might seem just a funny faux pas, but he didn't speak to me for about three weeks after that, except to tell people what a sorry thing it was that would drink that old slop two at a time. It was a little less for Baker: his penalty for being caught with a beer was about two weeks of the silent treatment.

But my options were limited. More than one shot of hard stuff rarely agreed with me. So, not willing to abstain, I finally achieved a breakthrough of sorts.

We were in London for the Wembley country music festival. On our first night there, lots of jet-lagged Americans were in the lounge at the Royal Lancaster Hotel, up at 3 a.m. because it was 9 p.m. at home. I ordered an ale and fired up a cigarette. No sooner had the waiter set the bottle in front of me than Bill appeared, standing over me. "I see you're drinkin' that old slop," he said.

"No, sir," I replied, "It's not beer."

"Sht! That's that old slop!"

"No, sir!" I said, turning the bottle around to show him the label. "It's Worthington's Pale Ale."

"Sht!"

Then, proving I could never peg him, he sat down and ordered a glass of wine.

I explained to him that people in Wisconsin drink a lot of beer and it's no big deal. With all the German, Polish, Scandinavian, and Irish folks, you'd find beer everywhere, even at a church picnic. My dad always told me I'd be better off laying off the hard stuff.

I guess I just wore Bill down. Months later, he could even joke about it. "That boy loves to drink that ol' slop, man, he gets 'em two at a time."

One night, riding into Pittsburgh—postsurgery, perhaps feeling his meds kicking in—he seemed particularly jovial. He had some homemade wine, which is the type he liked best, the sweeter the better, and he was passing it out in little Dixie cups. Handing me a cup, he said, "Now go easy on that, boy. 'Cause I know how it affects you, affects you, affects you."

After the show we went out to a restaurant. Bill went off to the dining room and had a steak. He was surrounded by women, happy as a clam. I sat at the bar, had a beer and a burger and another beer, talking baseball with the bartender. Afterward, standing out on the street waiting for the bus to be brought around, Bill was laughing and comparing me to (ex–Blue Grass Boy banjo player) Lamar Grier. "He's just like Lamar, just as quiet as he can be, don't hardly say nothin', but he has a couple of beers and then he wants to be everybody's friend, 'Why hello! My name is Mark! It's good to *meet* you!'"

HANGOVER MANAGEMENT 22

(recollected)

As much as Monroe despised drunkenness, over decades of leading a band he adopted a worldly pragmatism about it. With so many musicians having run through his band, he knew it was likely that his Boys would go out carousing. His personal opinion aside, as long as they could handle themselves he didn't worry about it too much.

But in the morning after a night before, he did delight in making someone who was feeling miserable feel even worse.

For example, one night in San Francisco, Butch got a snootful and decided he would go give Bill a piece of his mind. As I recall Butch's description, he went to Monroe's hotel room, knocked on the door, and leaned against the jamb to steady himself, head down. When Monroe opened the door, Butch, head still bowed, went into a five- or ten-minute monologue about what he thought and how he thought things should be. Monroe stood and listened, and when Butch had finished, Bill said, "Well, alright then," and without another word closed the door.

The next morning, while we were waiting in the lobby for the bus to be brought around, Butch was hunkered down on a couch, arms folded and a ball cap pulled low over his eyes. Monroe stepped out of the elevator, came up behind the couch, and, reaching over, lifted up Butch by his jaws and shook him, hollering, "HOW'S THAT HEAD TODAY, BOY?"

Another time on the West Coast, perhaps on the same trip, I went out and tied one on. I got back to the motel in the wee hours, but we had the next day off. I planned on sleeping in.

I was awakened at 7:30 a.m. by an urgent knocking on the door. I could tell by its vigor that it had to be Monroe. Staggering out of bed, still in my underwear, I cracked opened the door and peered out from behind it, squinting in the morning light. It was Bill, alright. Standing behind him, Baker got one look at me and turned away, laughing.

"We're going to breakfast!" Monroe bellowed, loud enough to make me wince. Go on ahead, I said, I'm gonna sleep a while longer. "Alright, then," Monroe said as I slammed the door and flopped back on the bed.

About forty-five minutes later came the same pounding. Cursing under my breath, I went to the door and peered out.

"We're back!"

23 ROAD JOURNAL, FEBRUARY 1980

(archival)

Midnight, Wednesday, February 27

I arrive at the bus to begin a trip, open the lower bay where I usually stow my bass, and find the bay is filled with record albums. Hundreds of albums!

We haven't carried any of Bill's records on the road since shortly after I joined last summer, but now they are all here and my responsibility: twenty-two titles and corresponding cassette tapes. It took me about fifteen minutes to rearrange everything, repacking and consolidating boxes, to make space for my bass.

Thursday, February 28

Morning, somewhere in Arkansas headed west on I-40, out of gas. Two farmers who happen along are more than proud to fuel up Mr. Bill Monroe.

We are bound for Muskogee, Oklahoma. The driver, Bill Aldrich, is generally a humorless redneck, but now he is fit to be tied. He's outside, trying to prime up the engine, when Wayne comes off the bus and asks whether we're in Missouri yet. "What the goddam hell would we be doing in Missouri!" he barks, missing the joke.

Tonight a woman buys eighty dollars worth of albums on the condition that she be introduced to Bill. Of course, Bill will greet any fan. She cries when she meets him.

Friday, February 29

On the way to Durant, Oklahoma, Aldrich gets on the CB radio to ask where he can find a truck stop. Someone replied there was one just down the road. We were just looking for lunch, but Aldrich had to see a *truck stop*. We drove clear over to Texas (at least a thirty-mile detour) before he spotted one where you could see the parked trucks from the highway. As usual, the food was horrible.

Saturday, March 1

We are checked into the Starlite Motel, the finest Many, Louisiana, has to offer. At breakfast I read a bit of the local newspaper. The name of the town made for some confusing sentences and headlines: "Many police baited the trap," "Many residents . . ." etc. Pronounced with a short *a*, Many is named for a Colonel Many of nearby Fort Jesup—so I guess they can't just change it to clear things up.

It's unseasonably cold, even brief flurries of snow. This is alarming to people who live south of Shreveport, so the weather scared Many off and we played for fifty to one hundred people.

On this night in Nashville there is a live national broadcast of the Grand Ole Opry. If we had stayed in Nashville I could have worked one night in town and made $100 more than I will tonight.

Sunday, March 2

El Dorado, Arkansas. Another poor turnout, but this time on a beautiful day, possibly pointing to advertising deficiencies.

This really gets Monroe down. His drawing power is still strong, but he's seen lean times before and he still gets worried. He recalled touring with Uncle Dave Macon years ago and said when the crowd was big Macon would say, "Yeah, ol' Uncle Dave can still bring 'em in," and if the crowd was off, he'd say, "Bill, it don't look like you're drawing near like you used to."

The band sounded like shit. Baker was stomping around, and at one point we had some words. After one number, which was too fast, I went over and said, "What's the matter? Wasn't that fast enough for you?"

Baker fired back. "Not fast enough? Goddam! . . ." etc. By now the applause had died down, and here we were with Baker giving me an earful for all to hear. Wayne walked over and said, "Ah, boys, we're on*stage!*" Afterward I heard Wayne saying, "Baker, what the hell is the matter with you?" It was a demoralizing evening.

Later, at yet another truck stop, Monroe had just been served when we heard the phone ring. He looked up from his plate and said, "It's probably the doctor calling to see if this here came out alright," and held up a six-inch-long hair he had just picked off his chicken.

Late that night I got Bill to talk a little about the old days. Coming up on Memphis, I thought of Elvis and asked whether he had ever played the Opry after all. He had, despite Acuff famously telling Presley he ought to go back to driving a truck.

"They was all scared of him," Bill said. "They was scared of a new sound. They was scared of me when I first come on there. Why, they'd never heard anything like that. All of them was playing in G, C, D, nothing else. They wasn't but a couple of men who could fiddle in different keys. No one went up the neck at all. But pretty soon they was all playing my stuff. People come on singing quartets, and they never done that much before. They'd all come on my show and do my stuff.

"It was the same with Elvis. They didn't want to let him in, they was scared for themselves. And the same thing happened with him. Pretty soon they was all doing his stuff.

"I thought he was good. He had his own style of singing, and I was glad to hear him take one of my songs and put his own style on it. He could really sing, boy. He could sing good gospel. He was told he had to have his own sound, so that's what he did."

Elvis put "Blue Moon of Kentucky" on the flip side of "That's All Right Mama." He personally thanked Bill for writing "Blue Moon." For his part, Monroe changed his own arrangement to add an upbeat two-four section to the back end of the original waltz, a tip of the hat to Presley.

Anyway, it was a tough trip, but Bill and James were real happy with the record sales for the weekend. It was $885 over four days of poor attendance. I guess the records are part of my job now.

(recollected)

With my baby face and slight build, and no service time on the traditional bluegrass circuit, I was regarded as a pretty green kid—even though I'd been playing professionally and touring the country for about five years when Monroe hired me.

So, Bill was mystified when we would go somewhere and I would know people there. I hadn't been anywhere, as far as he knew, yet here were my friends at a show in New Jersey (hometown buddies who drove out from Brooklyn), Chicago (friends down from Milwaukee), Kansas City and Denver (relatives), Seattle and Dallas (old bandmates), or San Francisco (my sister). It just didn't make sense to him, and inexplicable things really bothered him. "Everywhere we go, there's some long-haired thing comes around and says, 'Mark! How *are* you?'" he would say, shaking his head.

The matter got more serious in August 1980, when Monroe and Doc Watson played for President Carter's Georgia Barbecue on the South Lawn of the White House.

We had played in New Hampshire the night before, and a fan, having heard we would see the president the next day, told me to tell Carter he thought Senator Byrd (D-WV) was a lousy fiddle player. Indeed, with the Democratic National Convention approaching and Carter's popularity polls dropping, the "Fiddling Senator" was touting Ted Kennedy as a draft nomination. I told the man I would pass along his message if I got the chance.

We went to the White House that afternoon for a sound check, and while we were out on the stage, Carter came around to greet the band, shaking hands with each of us.

When I shook his hand I said, "Mr. President, last night a fellow up in New Hampshire asked me to tell you he thinks Senator Byrd is a lousy fiddle player."

Carter laughed and asked me what I thought. "I agree with him," I said. "How long did it take you to figure that out?" he asked. "Well, Mr. President, I'm a professional. I'm paid to know these things right away," I said. Carter giggled and said, "Well, I agree with you," then jumped from the front of the stage and walked toward the West Wing.

That night, at the close of the show, Carter came onstage to make some closing remarks. When he had finished, he left the lectern and headed offstage. With the crowd still applauding, he paused at the top of the steps and turned toward the band. Bill snapped to attention to acknowledge the president, but Carter looked past him and pointed at me.

"And I agree with what you said this afternoon!" he called out, then cackled and left the stage.

Bill glared at me. Baker laid a hand on my back and pushed me along, saying, "Don't even look at him, son, just keep moving," as we filed offstage.

25 NO, REALLY, WHO THE HELL *IS* THAT GUY?

(recollected)

Once we got into New York City, Franz had some trouble finding Lincoln Center. I rode shotgun as we rolled through Manhattan, goading Franz down Broadway past three movie houses named "Lincoln Center Theater."

Better get on the CB, Franz thought. "Any truckers out there can tell me where that Lincoln Center's at? Ten-four, buddy, hey you got an address on that? They didn't give me no address."

When we finally arrived, I had a hell of a time convincing Franz. "Look, it says Avery Fisher Hall, man!" he said.

"No, really, it's Lincoln Center. Avery Fisher Hall is a part of Lincoln Center, we're here. I've seen pictures of it," I assured him.

When we walked through the stage door, the security guard looked up from his desk.

"Bill Monroe band?"

"Yessir," Bill said.

"I have a telegram here for a Mark Hembree."

Bill stepped aside and looked at me. "That's me," I said, and took the telegram. A former bandmate and longtime friend (in fact, he would be best man at my wedding), Rich Ziven, had been on his way down from New England to see the show. But when he stopped to get gas, a cat had crawled under the hood. Unfortunately (especially for the cat), when Rich started his car, the stowaway thoroughly gummed up the works.

"Can't make show STOP cat broke my car STOP sorry STOP."

I was pondering this message when I realized Bill was still standing there, staring at me. "It's from a friend of mine," I said. "He's telling me he can't be here. Some kind of car trouble." Bill rolled his eyes.

That night there'd be no missing a meal after the show, no reason to fire up the bus and go hunting a truck stop. After the concert, standing out in front of Lincoln Center on the corner of Broadway and Sixty-Fifth at about 10:30 p.m. on a Friday night, Monroe looked around and said, "Boy, I'm awful hungry. Reckon anything's open?"

"Why, yeah, Boss," I said. "I'm sure we can find something. What do you want?"

PART IV
"HEAVY TRAFFIC AHEAD"

(partly archival)

Touted as the Bluegrass Music Festival of the United States, a three-day festival sponsored in large part by Kentucky Fried Chicken was held in downtown Louisville on the Belvedere, a plaza on the banks of the Ohio River, right behind the Galt House Hotel. The venue was terrific; backstage was a conference room in the Galt, air-conditioned, carpeted, no mud to wade through, no chiggers, and plenty of food and cold drinks nearby. It was luxurious for any bluegrass festival.

The festival was held in September, which took the edge off the Louisville heat. It was also around Bill's birthday, the thirteenth, and as a Kentucky patriarch he was showered with honors and awards and birthday gifts.

I enjoyed the musical lineup, with bands like the Whites, Hot Rize, New Grass Revival—pretty progressive for a show headlined by Bill Monroe.

Monroe didn't care for that kind of stuff. "Why, they've got people here that're no more bluegrass than the man in the moon! Buck White, shhh! Hot Rize, now there's a bluegrass band for you. Sht!"

Monroe's estimation of Hot Rize may have been influenced by Peter Wernick, Dr. Banjo, playing banjo through a phase shifter, a wah-wah effect that was not Bill's idea of how a banjo should ring. And Baker opined that the band's comic alter ego, the western band Red Knuckles and the Trailblazers, was the better group. Listening to Tim O'Brien sing the Lefty Frizzell number "Always Late," Baker said, "Now, by God, there's the shit they oughta be doing."

But I was glad to hang out with those fellas, acquaintances from a few years before in Colorado, and Jerry Douglas, who was playing with the Whites.

And we had a ball! Jerry mentioned that as a condition of the earlier-than-expected demise of Boone Creek (formed after Jerry and Ricky Skaggs left J. D. Crowe), Rounder Records had requested that he and Skaggs each do an album to satisfy their commitment. Jerry did his right away, but Ricky, who had signed with Sugar Hill Records and taken a gig with Emmylou Harris, still hadn't gotten around to it. We had a lot of laughs suggesting what sort of innovative format or theme Ricky might introduce. Wernick suggested *Ricky Skaggs Sings Songs of Africa*.

Anyway, the Louisville festival was terrific—huge crowds, comfortable accommodations. And it was easy to play: we finished on Sunday afternoon and headed straight home to Nashville, only three and a half hours away. Butch stayed behind and hung with Sam Bush, and we went back without him.

Naturally, the guy missing is always the one that gets ripped, especially if he's off with a hip guy like Sam. Bill said he was getting a headache and asked whether I had any BC (a powdered aspirin I'd never seen before I moved to the South). No, I said, but I think Butch might have some in his bunk.

Bill shook his head. "Sht! I don't want none of that powder, boy!"

Jerry Douglas and I actually met through our wives. His wife, Vicki, was the manager of a Waldenbooks store at RiverGate Mall in Goodlettsville, Tennessee. Not long after Georgia moved to Nashville, she and Vicki met during a show at the Station Inn. Georgia mentioned she was looking for work, and Vicki needed help at the store.

She told Jerry she had just hired someone whose husband had just gone to work for Monroe. When Georgia mentioned I needed some help moving the massive trailer I had bought for the move, Vicki volunteered Jerry to give me a hand. We began palling around, golfing during the week at a little three-par course near where they lived in a mobile home. Ricky Skaggs's VW Bug had been parked outside their trailer for months, while he was touring with Emmylou.

While we were in Louisville, Jerry had a great story for me about Ricky—and my dad.

Skaggs was traveling with Harris's band on a plane bound for Chicago. He was wearing a T-shirt from the Winfield National Flatpicking Contest, and when a middle-aged man noticed the shirt and asked him what band he was in, Skaggs, ever the wise guy, answered in his best Monroe voice, "Uh, Bill Monroe and the Blue Grass Boys."

Of course, he couldn't have known he was talking to my father. It was a fat pitch for Dad to swing at, and he didn't miss. "Well, son of a gun!"

he said. "What a coincidence! You must know my son, Mark Hembree. He plays bass in your band."

Skaggs looked stunned. The rest of the band fell out laughing. "Oh! I know Mark!" he said.

One time, someone had the medicine for Ricky.

TAKING MY TIME CAPSULES 27

(archival)

I hear it all the time: "I saw Mr. Bill for the first time back in . . .," as they recall the burly country boy with a full head of curly black hair, singing and playing his hard-charging music and leading a ferocious band.

In the 1940s, Bill was the hottest draw in country music. ("Bluegrass" had not yet been named; the line between it and "country" had not yet been drawn. It was all hillbilly music.) Monroe remembers gigs in countless small towns like Galax and Staunton, Virginia; Waynesboro, Tennessee; the Carolinas; and "all across the Southland," as he would say, where the crowds lined up hours ahead of time, two or three times around a city block, waiting in the rain.

These images flash briefly before the conversation digresses to the cars, wages, and prices of those days, memories conjured by Bill and his music. "Why, I worked fifty-five hours and made $12.50 a week. I had a brand-new car and a girl on every corner!" one old-timer told me.

Now, at this show, there was a Model T pickup truck stuck in a pothole, and I had to go help push it out. Just like my forebears in the old days, I heaved and hoed, and the wheels threw mud in my face.

Butch asked me when I joined the band, "Are you ready to live in the 1930s? I mean, are you really ready to do that?"

I'm finding out what he meant. And I don't know anybody who is.

28 JOHN DUFFEY

(archival)

In the early 1960s, the Country Gentlemen—Charlie Waller, Eddie Adcock, Tom Gray, and John Duffey—were one of the first of a new generation of bluegrass bands. It wasn't quite "newgrass," but it was progressive in its repertoire and instrumental innovation. Waller's lead voice and the harmonies were more palatable to a wider audience, vocally more like the Limeliters than like Lester Flatt. Working out of the DC area, the band was perfectly positioned to ride the crest of the folk wave that was creating a new, bigger audience for bluegrass.

In those days, Monroe remained stern and unyielding as he maintained the integrity of his own style—and he still wasn't accepting variations of the genre he had created. By all accounts, this bothered Duffey not one whit. He was a strong mandolin player, sang with a powerful tenor, and saw no reason to take a back seat to Bill. Duffey would bend notes and look straight at Monroe. (I heard a story that Bill, once back on the bus, was fooling around on the mandolin, bending notes like Duffey.)

However, whatever enmity may have existed eventually turned into shtick. Duffey would show up and razz Bill, and if they shared a stage it was comedy. Duffey rivals Bill physically as well—though, even in his seventies, Big Mon cuts quite a figure.

A typical encounter: Duffey, unannounced, strides to center stage and swaps his ball cap for Monroe's Stetson. Bill says, "Uh, what are you doing out here?"

"I figured your show wasn't going so great, thought you needed some help," Duffey replies. "What do you want to hear me play?"

"How about 'Old Joe Clark'?" Bill says.

"Is that the only song you know?" says Duffey.

"I thought that's the only one you could play," says Bill.

They launch into it, playing harmony, and when his turn comes, Duffey calls out, "You want to hear a Monroe break?"

And so forth. But the real fireworks went off when they sang, blasting the two highest-caliber tenors in the business into each other's face at point-blank range. Standing between them and singing baritone, Butch rolled his eyes and buckled at the knees.

"I ain't afraid of the old man," Duffey would say.

One more fond memory of Duffey: when we played a show at the White House with the Seldom Scene during the Carter years, I marveled at his setting up a leatherette cocktail kit on a planter wall near the South Portico and mixing himself a whiskey sour.

Duffey does not worry about what anybody thinks.

ON TO POCATELLO! 29

(partly archival)

It had been a long few days to get as far west as Limon, Colorado, where we pulled up for fuel and supper. A truck driver came over and wanted Bill's autograph. We found out we were both headed for Pocatello, Idaho. He was glad to find out about us playing there, and said he would come to the show. But for now he was going to lay up and get a shower and nap before going on.

Later that night, coming down the mountains into Laramie, Wyoming, we ran into some icy spots and steadily increasing snowfall. Our driver, Franz, was from Southern Indiana and not experienced on snow. Despite some gentle prodding from me, he would not go above forty, even when we got to lower elevation and the snow turned to slush (but not yet frozen). It didn't help that he was slaphappy as hell from being too long behind the wheel.

We spent an hour and a half of indecision at a truck stop in Laramie—where was the snow coming from, how bad was it, will you let Wayne drive, you're too tired? I could see by the radar on TV that it was coming from the northwest, and it looked like a doozy. I told Franz if we didn't get the hell out of Laramie we might spend the next few days here.

So on we went, Franz still poking along at forty. I went back to the bunks and woke Wayne. Years before, when he lived in Ohio, he had driven trucks for Schneider Lines, based in Green Bay, Wisconsin. I told him what I had seen on the radar, and said if we didn't step it up and go we might get stranded out on the plains.

By that time Baker was roused. "By God, now, they'll come along and find us like them cattle with our legs stickin' out of the damn snow," he said. That's right, I said, we've gotta beat this storm.

Wayne came up front, and after about a half hour of cajoling he convinced Franz to give up the wheel and get some sleep. After that, Wayne punched it up to about sixty and set about the serious business of pushing west across those bare plains, where the wind turns a half inch of snow into smooth, slippery glass. Out there, everything is remote. Slide off the road? Tell it to the hills and rocks.

I went back to my bunk and turned in. A few hours later I awoke. We were still rolling along, though we had slowed. In the back of the bus, just over the rear wheels, I could tell the snow had deepened, muffling the whine of the tires, and that it was plenty slick. I could hear Wayne and Kenny up front, Wayne calling "Whoa, mule!" as the Silver Eagle fishtailed a little here and there. But we made it through.

By the time we headed north into Idaho, the sun was shining and the storm was behind us. We checked in at Pocatello and had the luxury of a night's rest before the show the next night.

At the concert, we saw the driver we had met back in Colorado two nights before. Having stopped for a nap in Limon, he'd been stuck on the wrong side of that storm. He had just arrived in town, with barely enough time to clean up and head for the hall to see the show.

30 ROOMS/NO ROOMS

(archival)

We finished working in Seattle about midnight and drove a half mile to the motel where we had reservations. The rates were thirty-eight dollars for a double, thirty for a single. Baker left the front desk and got back on the bus, raising hell about the prices. So, we left.

The search was on. "Now, little as you think about it," as Baker says, this makes a lot of sense. You take a Silver Eagle bus and drive around the city at about one in the morning hoping to find rooms for six people without reservations. This works especially well on a weekend night.

The object of this game: find a motel with two doubles and two singles for twenty dollars or less per room. You have until about 2:30 a.m., at which time the Boss goes to his midbus berth and closes the door, signaling the end of play. The band sleeps on the bus and is penalized in the morning: no shower, and if the sun is shining, you wake up in a pool of your own juices.

This can occasionally be embarrassing, like the time in DC when Bill was to be honored by the Smithsonian with a concert at the White House.

We were in town the night before, once again searching in vain for vacancies at an acceptable rate, but when we pulled up at a motel, the diesel engine suddenly went into a runaway—throttle stuck wide open, engine screaming. Donald, the driver then, was a smooth-talking Georgian and a crack-shot mechanic, but now he was frantic, stamping the accelerator, then sprinting back to the rear of the bus, throwing open the engine compartment and banging on linkages with his bare hands, then running up front again to kick the fuel pedal. We sat there in the front lounge as the rpm continued to spool up. "By God, she's gonna blow!" Baker cried. Monroe paced and wrung his hands, his eyes flashing like dollar signs on a cash register. Finally, whatever Donald was doing took. The engine wound down as he slumped over the wheel, gasping, his wavy pompadour hanging over his face.

That was all too much for Bill. Emotionally spent, he went to his room and slammed the door. We would go no farther that night.

The next day we went to Ralph Rinzler's house to shower and shave before proceeding to the White House.

The room search can be a dangerous game if you're playing the wrong position. Shotgun is the hot seat, because a wrong word or a bad attitude can make you the recipient of all the frustration and anger of bandmates, a tired driver, or Monroe.

The safest place to be at times like that is the back of the bus, out of earshot and out of sight. In San Diego, I watched from my bunk as an indecisive driver passed several motels (I counted eight from my side of the bus) before settling on a Motel 6.

When the bus stopped, Butch, in the opposite bunk, rolled over and asked, "Are we there?"

"Hard to tell," I said. Just then the engine shut down. "We're either there or we're broke down."

Butch took this answer as an indication that I had effectively assimilated the proper Blue Grass Boy attitude. Assume nothing until you see the room key.

31 | OF GLOVES AND BANANAS

(recollected)

If an Opry spot ended or began a week's tour, band members who didn't live in town either got a motel or stayed with somebody in town. Butch lived in Radford, Virginia, but if he needed a place to crash in Nashville on the weekend he might stay at my apartment. So it was when we came home from a trip early one Saturday morning.

Butch helped me brush the snow off my crummy little Vega. He was wearing a pair of fine, kid leather driving gloves. With the defroster blasting hot air, he laid them up on the dashboard to dry.

Now here is where I must diverge to backfill this story. Sometime before I was in the band, Baker had pulled a practical joke meant to influence Butch's use of the small refrigerator on the bus.

Baker kept a couple of things in there—maybe a mason jar or two of pickled vegetables—to augment his snacks of Ritz crackers and Vienna sausages (pronounced vah-EN-nee). Butch might bring a grocery bag of stuff, mostly fruit and vegetables, but when he put a bunch of bananas in the fridge, Baker felt he was taking up too much space.

He told Butch he shouldn't put those bananas in the refrigerator, it would cause them to turn black and spoil. Butch didn't take the hint.

So, when Baker had the chance, he noted the size and number of the bananas, then went out and bought the ripest, blackest equivalent bunch of bananas he could find and swapped them out.

Butch went to the fridge to get a banana and was appalled at how rapidly they had spoiled. Baker expressed his sympathy as Butch threw away the rest of the bunch.

Eventually the ruse was revealed, and Butch learned he'd been had.

Now back to the gloves. Having laid them up on the dashboard, Butch forgot them there. I switched cars to drive to the Opry that night, and Butch headed home after the show. The gloves were still up on the Vega's dash, sun-drying under the windshield, as the weather improved. A few days later, I spotted them and was shocked to see they had shrunk until they were barely bigger than the palm of my hand.

I brought them with me on the band's next trip out. Back in the bunks, stowing our stuff, I told Butch I had found his driving gloves. He was delighted. He had been wondering where the hell he had put them, they were pretty expensive. I apologized and told him I'd forgotten them, too, and that they'd been sitting under the windshield for a few days, baking in the sun. Then I presented the shrunken gloves.

Butch's face fell. He snatched them out of my hand, flung them to the floor, and stalked off, muttering, "Fucking bananas!"

Mystified, I turned and looked at Baker, who exploded in laughter. Then he told me the rest of the story.

PUSHING THE BUS UP CUMBERLAND GAP 32

(recollected)

It's always a steep climb through the Cumberland Gap, but it gets harder to gain altitude when it's snowing like it was after the show this night as we crossed the mountains back to Kentucky and Tennessee.

Donald, an experienced, smooth driver, was carefully guiding the bus up the mountain. Sensing the road surface, he called out, "Boys, she's starting to slip." We could hear the engine race a little when it did.

"You need us to push?" Wayne called back.

Now, a Silver Eagle bus is thirty-seven feet long and weighs about fourteen tons.

"Push?" I asked, thinking he was kidding. I'd pushed cars out of snowbanks before. But a bus?

Wayne explained that just a little push could help the bus gain enough traction to stop slipping. "If you can get going, keep going," Wayne told Donald. "We'll meet you at the top."

Donald laughed. "I ain't stoppin'!" He slowed to a crawl, and Wayne, Butch, and I, still in our suits, stepped off and went to the back of the bus. It was southern-style snow—wet, slushy, and quick to ice. As Donald eased the throttle up and the wheels began to spin, we pushed, not easy to do on slush when you're wearing dress shoes.

But wonder of wonders, the tires began to grip a little. We kept pushing, and sure enough, the bus found its footing and began to roll forward. Now we were trotting after it. "Keep going!" Wayne yelled, waving Donald on.

The bus was still creeping forward, and I decided, even though Donald was picking up speed, I could still sprint to the front door, slippery shoes and all.

Donald saw me coming and threw open the door. In the final kick of my sprint, I leapt onto the bottom step, catching the grab handle there and pulling myself aboard, laughing.

Donald was about the age of my father, and now the look he gave me reminded me of Dad after I'd done something stupid.

"If you'd missed, you'd have gone under the front wheel," he said, "That is, if you hadn't already slipped and gone under one of the other wheels first."

Young and immortal, I had not thought of that until then.

At the top of the pass, we pulled aside, and Wayne and Butch, who had caught a ride up the hill with one of the cars trailing behind us, came back aboard.

After a few laughs, Wayne gave me the same bawling out.

PART V
"MY LAST DAYS ON EARTH"

(recollected)

The live album *Bean Blossom '79* was recorded just a couple of weeks before I auditioned for the band. The record didn't come out until after I joined, and it set a high standard for me. The band was tight, and Randy Davis sounded great on the bass. I had hoped that once I had my bearings I would be able to live up to the job.

I had good reason to doubt it—Randy was chosen by Kenny Baker, had played with Monroe for five years, and was as solid as they come—and the Boys often reminded me of it. When Wayne, Kenny, and Butch all recorded their own albums in 1980, none of them asked me to play. Butch and Wayne used Randy. Baker used Roy Huskey, one of the go-to session guys in Nashville. Those were great players, and I did not count among them.

So, I had no reason to think that if and when Bill decided to record another album he would use me on it. In any event, I was not in the loop and not aware of any plans.

When we did record in February 1981, it was on short notice. I had no idea of what was planned for the album or to what degree I would be involved. I didn't even know until we got in the studio that it would be the first instrumental album Bill had recorded since *Bill Monroe's Uncle Pen* in 1972. It was only the third instrumental album of his career.

I did know some of the tunes, though. Bill would occasionally pull one out of his hat as we were warming up for a show, and I became familiar with a few of them. We sometimes performed one of them on a show—"Evening Prayer Blues," by DeFord Bailey, "Lochwood," "Ole Ebenezer Scrooge," and "Come Hither to Go Yonder," the title of which was misstated on the album cover (along with my name). I heard some of the other tunes for the first time there in the studio.

The biggest surprise came when Bill, calling the next tune to record, said, "Last Days on Earth." The other Boys laid down their instruments and headed out of the room. I started to follow, but Bill said, "No, no, no, you stay."

I was standing there wondering what was going on when Norman Blake came into the room. "Hey, Norman!" I said, glad to see him but now even more mystified. We exchanged pleasantries, and he sat down and took out his guitar. He looked up at me, smiling a little.

"You don't know what we're doing, do you?" he said.

I told him I didn't, and he smiled more.

"It's called 'My Last Days on Earth,'" he said.

"OK," I said. "Time signature?"

"Three-four," he said.

"Key?" I asked.

Norman giggled. "D-flat minor."

"What?" Now Norman was chuckling, shaking his head.

I had never played anything in D-flat before, and, aside from this number, I haven't since.

The reason for the key was the strange "split-string" tuning Bill had come up with when he wrote it. Normally, a mandolin is tuned like a violin but with four pairs of strings, each pair tuned alike. In split-string tuning, one or more of each pair is tuned to a different pitch for various effects. Organs have stops for "mutations." This tuning was something like that.

Monroe had recorded "Get Up John" with split-string tuning. But this one was more involved. Larry Sledge was there at Bill's home when he played it for some friends, and Bill asked him to remember the tuning. Larry wrote it down and would come around every so often to retune the mandolin for him.

None of that was helping me. I tried tuning my bass down half a step to play as if in C, but that didn't sound good. Tuning up a half step was no help, either. So I practiced a little and found a way to do it, playing as little as possible, and we recorded the basic tracks.

I didn't hear it again until the album came out. It was the last cut, so I listened through the album and wondered what must have happened in the mixing sessions. There were strange things. Most album recordings have at least one session for fixes, giving the players a chance at repairs, but not this one. Displeased with part of a banjo break, Bill had them turn off the banjo in that spot, not giving Butch another crack at it and not replacing it but simply letting the rest of the tracks proceed sans banjo—a blank spot "compensated" for by dialing up a goofy reverberation effect on the mandolin. Ironically, the tune was called "Fair Play."

Finally, the last cut—beginning with the sound of ocean surf and seagulls (what?), as if Rod McKuen was about to recite something. Then came the chimes, Bill playing a series of harmonics as the intro. Now came orchestral strings and a choral arrangement, which made Bill's mandolin sound all the more atonal. And finally, as the sound of surf and seagulls returned, there came the signatory harmonics again, and a slow, dramatic retard as the last chimes were repeated. It reminded me of the very end of Richard Strauss's "Also Sprach Zarathustra" (the beginning of which is the opening theme in the film *2001: A Space Odyssey*)—the closing notes slowing to a stop, like a pulse ceasing.

I was dumbfounded. Confounded. Strings? A chorus? Seagulls and surf? It was the strangest recording by Monroe since the tom-tom and echo-chamber Indian chant at the beginning of "Cheyenne." And this was stranger than that. I had been a part of history—really weird history.

"My Last Days on Earth" was released as a single, and Bill wanted to play it on shows. None of the others could or would play in D-flat, so Bill and I performed it alone. Eventually I got better at playing it, but it was always scary for me.

But, then, it *was* a scary tune. One night in Beckley, West Virginia, we played it pretty well. Monroe was casting a spell, and as he played the eerie, final chimes, the audience seemed to be holding its breath. Somewhere in the house a baby whimpered, "Mama!" This juxtaposition of an infant in arms and an old man at the edge of an abyss reminded me not of Strauss's musical motif but of the surreal end of *2001*.

On the bus after the show, I brought it up with Bill. He had heard it, too. I said, "Man, that really spooked me. That baby came right in there, like what that number is really about."

"Yessir," Bill agreed.

It was a prime example of Bill's mystic side. Those harmonics, the chimes, were the beginning and the end, birth and death. Bill's soul was in the middle.

Many years later, I chanced to meet mandolin player Joe Clark at a show in Wisconsin. He told me that when he was twelve, he and his dad's band had opened for us in a show at the high school in Abingdon, Virginia.

Dana Cupp (who would play banjo with Bill a few years after I left) had given young Joe a cassette of Bill playing "Ole Ebenezer Scrooge." Joe had taken it home and played the song for weeks, trying to get it right. Now, nervous before the big show, he sat alone backstage, playing it again and again.

As Joe was bent over his mandolin, a pair of perfectly polished shoes came into his field of vision. Without even looking up, he knew who it was.

But he was afraid to look up. He finished playing the tune before finally raising his face to look at Monroe.

"Uh, there's a wrong note in there," Bill said, and held out his hands for the mandolin. Joe passed it to him, and he played the tune through, then passed the mandolin back.

Then Monroe stood back and clasped his hands behind his back. "Now tell me, son, how did you come to hear that number?" he asked.

This was an excellent question, because the album had not yet been released. Not wanting to get Dana in trouble, the quick-thinking twelve-year-old lied. "I guess I heard you play it on a show somewhere," he said.

Recalling the story years later, Joe grinned. "Don't you know that gave me a leg up with the old man!" he said. Monroe was really impressed by Joe being able to hear a tune at a show, then go home and play it. I'm sure Dana was glad the story ended that way, too.

34 BACK IN THE SADDLE

(archival)

Lying in my bunk and looking out the window on the other side, I watch the countryside go by in a blur, forming horizontal bands of dark and light greens, occasionally broken by vertical lines of black and patches of red-orange. Having relearned the nation from this point of view, I can tell by the colors we are in Georgia.

This is Bill's first trip out after a two-month absence following an operation for colon cancer. He had entered the hospital secretly—I discovered I was out of a job (at least temporarily) three days after his admission, not long after we recorded *Master of Bluegrass*.

When the news did get out, his room was besieged by fans, associates, friends, preachers, mourners, you name it. One day there were more than one hundred visitors.

The scene in and around the room was funeral, a mood amplified by the southern affinity for death and tragedy that imbues so many lyrics to so many country songs. And there were preachers of one sort or another coming and going throughout the day, doing their part to further charge the atmosphere with solemnity.

After the operation, there was more secrecy. Bill was carted from one room to another to avoid well-wishers so he could get well. I sneaked in the day after his surgery. Expecting to find his son James, or perhaps Wayne, I tiptoed into his room and found Bill sitting upright in bed, glaring at me just like old times.

The operation was cautiously rated a success. They removed a section of colon and a small, malignant growth. The prognosis was good.

The other night at the Opry, Bill had told Butch, "Learn these tunes note for note, exactly how they go, 'cause someday when I'm gone there won't be no one else who knows them." Butch said he had tears in his eyes.

Now we are back on the road, and a lulu of a trip it is: Montgomery on Friday night, Key West on Saturday, and then back to Nashville. Now, as I write this, we are passing Atlanta on our way back north. Bill has had some frail moments, and road food has been hard for him to digest (especially from the places where Franz chooses to stop), but I think he will get stronger as he goes. He always does.

It's the music. Nothing like the love of your life to make you feel better. And was there ever a greater trouper? He doesn't just rise to the occasion. He surpasses it.

You can see it in reverse when he leaves the stage. Once he's in the wings, out of sight, his shoulders drop, his head bows, and he becomes his old, aching self again—until next time.

MONROE HANGS TOUGH, BUT IT'S TOUGH 35

(partly archival)

After Monroe's operation, people who heard he had cancer wondered when or even if he would be able to go back to touring. But people who knew Monroe knew the answer to that question: he would be back in time for the next show.

As tough as the old man was, this was at his physical limits. Nothing he ate agreed with him, and digestion was painful and unpredictable. He suffered humiliating bouts of incontinence, awful for a man of his dignified carriage.

Rolling into Syracuse, New York, early enough to find lodging before the show, I was riding shotgun with Franz to mitigate his usual indecisiveness and find a motel. Franz was dithering, and I was trying to direct him, when Bill, no doubt in severe distress, started yelling at both of us—what's the matter with you stupid things, we need to find them rooms now, can't you do nothing right, and so on.

I barked back at Bill, "I can't steer this bus, I can't step on the brake for him."

That was the push we needed, though. "There!" I said, pointing at the next likely motel, and Franz pulled in.

About a half hour after we checked in, Butch and I sharing a room, Monroe knocked on the door. I answered, and Bill apologized for yelling at me, said he felt awful bad right then and we needed to get stopped. It's OK, I told him, I know you're not feeling good. Don't worry about it. But thanks.

After I closed the door I turned around, and Butch was standing there, eyes wide and mouth agape. He said in all his years he had never seen Bill apologize to anyone. No one ever had. He must really be in pain.

When we pulled up to the Landmark Theatre, Bill Knowlton, the show's host, met the bus. He said Baker took him aside to tell him Monroe was in bad shape. He would definitely have to rest during intermission if he was to play both sets.

After the first set, Knowlton took the stage to announce that Monroe was still recovering and would not be available for autographs as usual during intermission. Then he saw Monroe walking up the aisle to the lobby for the customary meet and greet. He was deathly pale, Knowlton recalled.

Monroe returned and played the second set. And the next night in Chautauqua, New York. And the next three days in Northern Ohio.

My wife-to-be took this photo in 1976 in Wisconsin.
It's still one of my favorites of Monroe. Photo by
Georgia Henes-Hembree.

Being introduced at the autumn Bean Blossom festival in 1980; getting the hang of
being a Blue Grass Boy. Left to right: Kenny, Butch, me, Bill, and Wayne.

To Mark Hembree,
Best Wishes,
Rosalynn Carter   Jimmy Carter

Being received for lunch at the White House in October 1979. *From left:* President Jimmy Carter, Rosalynn Carter, and some bass player from Wisconsin. Official White House photo, author's collection.

Albums $7.0
Tapes $8.0
Double Albums &
Tapes

The record shack at Bean Blossom, where I spent many hours selling albums, cassettes, T-shirts, coffee mugs, and sundries.

The Blue Grass Quartet on a perfect Sunday morning at Bean Blossom. *Left to right:* Bill, Blake, me, Wayne.

Kenny Baker barely accedes to a photo backstage at Bean Blossom. Doug Green's descriptive, *irascible*, is perfect.

Early morning, Baker riding shotgun. He'd stop playing swing after Bill got up.

Bill goes over the edge of a ravine to search for a stone to add to his Walkway of the States. If we were going through a state he didn't have in his collection, he'd watch for a wash or stream likely to yield a flat rock of the shape he wanted, then call for the driver to pull over.

In the music barn at Bean Blossom. Bill's vision was pretty poor without his glasses, so my putting on nose and glasses for the last number in the set threw him for a loop. The barn was a more informal venue where I could get by with a stunt like this. Photo by Rich Ziven.

My daughter, Katherine, meets Bill Monroe backstage at the Opry in 1982.

With Katie, Georgia, and almost Michael backstage at the Opry in winter 1984.

My roomie and good buddy Blake Williams and I at Bean Blossom. Uncle Birch's erstwhile refreshment stand is in the background.

Mule Day Parade, Columbia, Tennessee. It's not easy playing bass in a crosswind on a wagon being pulled by mules. Photo by Gerald Holly, courtesy of Carol Holly Hamby; author's collection.

At work at Bean Blossom, doing my job and trying to stay with Bill. Photo by Lee Bjorndal.

Monroe and
Baker arrive in
Honolulu.

Onstage at the Waikiki Shell. We went straight there from the airport for a sound check, checked into the hotel to shower and shave, then came back and hit the stage.

Close work at Great Gorge, New Jersey, 1981. Working a single vocal mike is not as easy as people might think. Until you get the hang of it, you might get run over. Photo by Peter Rowan.

Bill shows off a fine-looking mount in the Israeli countryside.

On the first country music tour of Israel, Bill was baptized in the Jordan River. It meant the world to him.

It wasn't every day you'd see Monroe riding a camel in Israel. King Wilkie was a famous horse of Bill's; I didn't catch the camel's name.

Wayne Lewis pauses for a camera shot, while Bill strides toward the Western Wall in Jerusalem. Blue Grass Boys were easy to pick out in the crowd there.

Bill and a monk share a moment near the Sea of Galilee in Israel.

BILL MONROE'S

10TH ANNUAL BLUE GRASS FESTIVAL

BEAN BLOSSOM, IND.

SATURDAY, JUNE 19, 1976

$7.00

THIS TICKET MUST BE WORN AT ALL TIMES

Ticket from one of my first trips to Bean Blossom, three years before I auditioned for Monroe. Not a bad lineup for seven dollars; a Saturday usually included such acts as Lester Flatt, Jim & Jesse, Ralph Stanley, the Osborne Brothers, Jimmy Martin, Del McCoury, Larry Sparks, J. D. Crowe, Carl Story, and more.

PART VI
"ROCKY ROAD BLUES"

(partly archival)

A commander stands before his troops and asks for a volunteer to step forward, and in unison all but one step back: that's more or less how I became Bill's de facto road manager. We had just gotten off a plane somewhere on the West Coast (Portland or Seattle, maybe?) and Bill asked who would drive the rental car. We all looked at one another, and somehow I was volunteered.

It turned out to be a blessing. We wound up in a compact station wagon with a fairly uncomfortable back seat, so Bill and I rode in relative comfort. And we had a lot of driving to do that week.

I also benefited from some not-so-dumb luck. We were to play a show at Caltech in Pasadena, and after a long ride down I-5 I guessed at an exit somewhere close to the center of town to find lunch and get a better idea of where we were. (Mind you, this was the early 1980s—no Google, no GPS, no cell phones.) I got off the highway (must have been I-210) and spotted what looked like a decent restaurant on Colorado Boulevard. I told the boys to go ahead and get a bite, I'd try to get some more directions and figure out where to stay.

As soon as Bill was out of sight, I walked across the lot to a liquor store and chatted up the cashier. He told me there was a Best Western on Colorado not far from there, and only a few blocks from Caltech. "You can see it from there," he said.

Turned out the restaurant was pretty good, and everyone was in a better mood when they got back. We piled into the wagon and drove a short bit, and I pulled into the motel lot and went in to get their rates. The price was OK with Bill, so we checked in. Coming out of the office, Bill asked how far it was to the show. I pointed down a street running south from there and said, "See those buildings at the end of the street? That's where we're playing, Caltech."

"You're kidding, boy!" Bill said, with the sort of delighted smile I rarely received from him. "We could walk there, couldn't we?" "Yes, sir," I said, "should be a nice evening for it."

Though he rarely passed them along, Bill had all the advance information and contacts (which certainly would have helped me). As it was, the people running the show were happy that we had found our way to that motel, which is where they had booked the Boys of the Lough, who were also on the show.

On the Boulevard of Roses, I had come out smelling like one.

We met out on the street that evening, and Bill looked rested and glad to be on foot. It was a great show, of course—Bill Monroe and the Boys of the Lough! Afterward, back at the motel, I met Aly Bain and we stayed up till the wee hours as we drank and he fiddled until we were both tipping over. By then I was playing guitar. "I love the way you Yanks keep time!" he said, begging to play another tune.

And on that trip I felt I had befriended Bill, too. On the morning we flew out, I had to run the borrowed string bass from Pasadena all the way over to McCabe's Guitar Shop in Santa Monica. Minus traffic, it's a forty-five-minute drive. Of course, I hit traffic. Fearful of making us late for our flight, I was hotfooting it down the freeway and got a speeding ticket for going sixty-eight miles per hour. *Sixty-eight!* "I guess I'm the only one you could catch up to," I grumbled. The patrolman admitted he wrote more tickets for over seventy than under. "Have a nice day," he said, handing me the ticket.

Back at the motel, Bill had been getting nervous. I apologized and told him I had done the best I could, even got a speeding ticket on the way back. He asked how much, then fished the cash out of his pocket and handed it to me.

"You see, you didn't even have to ask me for it!" he said. I might have asked, violating the Monroe code, but he didn't give me the chance.

At the airport, we cleared our bags out of the car, and in my anxiety, I momentarily lost track of the keys. I was rifling through my pockets and cursing, then came up with them. Bill laughed. "That's just like me. That's the way I do!"

From then on I was often the road gofer, passing out plane tickets, leading the way to boarding gates, seeing to the luggage, searching out restaurants.

Of the various episodes to follow, my favorite was leading Bill and the Boys through customs in Atlanta. Pairing an American Tourister garment valet with a Cassini carry-on bag (and not carrying a bass), I had no luggage to check. So, returning from London, I clapped on my Stetson (easier to wear than carry) and went to hold a place in line, while Bill and the Boys waited to claim their luggage.

With me at the front of the line was a dapper Frenchman who haughtily informed me that he was a diplomat and would be going first. I said nothing. But when the customs agent raised his hand and motioned to us, I strode forward. "But, but I am a diplomat!" the Frenchman sputtered. "Welcome to the USA, Jacques," I said, mangling the name with a hard J and tipping my hat.

The agent, an older fellow with a thick Georgia accent and a Lester Maddox face, asked where I'd been and what was my business. I told him I was a musician returning from a tour of Europe. Are there more members of your band here? he asked. "Yes, sir," I answered, "Bill Monroe and the Blue Grass Boys," and pointed to the baggage carousel where the others, wearing their Stetsons, were claiming their luggage.

"Is Mr. Bill here?" the agent asked, his voice rising. "Yes, sir," I said. "That's him in the white hat."

"Well, I'll be! It sure is! You reckon he'd sign something for me?"

"I'm sure he would," I said, waving the boys to come on. And here they came, Bill bringing up the rear, and the customs agent was beaming and telling Bill how many years he'd been listening to him. From there we sailed right through.

On the way out I glanced over my shoulder and saw the diplomat marching forward, infuriated, and the agent holding up his hand and nodding.

Having suffered the disdain of Frenchmen many times, I found it wonderfully satisfying.

WEST COAST ROUTING AND CANADIAN CUSTOMS 37

(archival)

We're out of the rooms early this morning, allowing twelve hours to drive the 144 miles from Seattle to Vancouver, British Columbia.

As usual, divining departure times has been tricky as plans are made at the drop of a hat and changed without notice. We consistently leave about a half hour before the agreed time. This morning we left without breakfast ("Uh, we've got to go, now," Bill says), passed at least six good-looking restaurants, and wound up at a Denny's ("We want a good place to park now, hear?").

As it turned out, we needed a little extra time at the Canadian border. When American musicians cross into Canada, sometimes—not every time—they have to declare their instruments and equipment and then pay a deposit. This is to discourage selling the stuff in Canada. The money is refunded when you get back to the States.

It's random and annoying, especially if it's unexpected. But on this crossing, it annoyed the Canadians more.

We were preceded at the border by some show band that carried a lot of equipment: sound, lights, the whole production. Canadian customs agents gave them a thorough going-over.

So, they were all warmed up when they got to us. We didn't have any stage equipment, just the instruments, and we all lowballed, following Baker's lead. He could have honestly told the guy his fiddle was priceless—especially if it really was a Guarnerius—but Baker, with a straight face, told the customs agent it was worth $200. I think Wayne and Butch were between $200 and $300 with their Martin guitar and Gibson banjo, respectively. I told the guy my Kay plywood bass was $400 ("because it's bigger," I explained).

Bill came last, and by that time the officer was already growing skeptical and a little testy. But when Bill—obviously the leader and, by dint of personal presence, obviously a big deal—told the guy his 1923 Gibson F-5 Lloyd Loar was worth $150, the guy blew.

"Do you mean to tell me an instrument like this is worth only $150?" he demanded.

Bill bored in, his voice rising. "That's what I give for it at a barber shop in Florida in 19 and 45. It was in the window there and I bought it from the man there and I never did get no receipt, I just shook hands with the man and he's dead now, so you'll just have to take my word on it!" Then, jaw set, he fixed his fearsome gaze on the agent and awaited the next question.

None was forthcoming. We wound up the paperwork pretty quickly after that and went on our way, chuckling all the way to Vancouver.

Then it was back down the coast again, another course of the yo-yo on this western tour. A few more dates in California this October: Davis (13), 500 miles then La Jolla (14), and 480 miles then San Jose (15). Then head northeast 2,000 miles and play Minneapolis on October 18, ride 700 miles southeast to Oberlin, Ohio, for October 20, and then make a 300-mile jaunt to Bean Blossom for the weekend before heading home. Sure glad no one at the booking agency has to make any of these trips.

Woke up this morning to overhear the maids discussing when to clean which rooms. "One, four, five, and nine do later; they're not leaving until five."

Ah, breakfast and a shower! Now I have a simple shortcut to planning my day, as opposed to the standard intelligence-gathering to find out when you're leaving and whether you have time to shit, shower, shave, and eat.

It's an understatement to say Bill's circadian rhythms are at odds with mine. His is a farmer's schedule, southern style. Up before dawn, massive breakfast, ready to kick ass by seven, dinner (not "lunch") about eleven thirty, and then, for Bill, not much to eat until after the show, which is usually after ten or eleven. Then a big meal and off to bed.

For me, this is an excellent way to pick up twenty or thirty pounds in no time.

However, these days, after surgery for colon cancer, Bill is off his feed. He's sleeping more, sometimes foggy and out of touch. Is he living out his Last Days on Earth? Is the reported success of the operation all a cover-up? The routing on this trip is brutal, and sometimes I hear Bill saying to fans, "If we get to come back."

Is he trying to pack it all in at the end? From November 13 until the twentieth it's essentially a 192-hour ride with breaks to eat and work. Why are they doing this to him? Better yet, why is he doing this to himself? Well, first, for the money. Of course, the people at Buddy Lee Attractions make money without having to endure this, but they are acting at Bill's behest—and he is a tough old bird.

Get up at dawn and get breakfast, then it's hammer down and no stopping until dinner. Thus we make our way across Nevada, Utah, Wyoming, Nebraska . . .

Now I'm at the front of the bus as we roll through Nebraska, watching nothing go by for miles and miles for the umpteenth time. Something about Ogallala—it's always either not far enough from where you left or too far away from where you're going.

38 ROAD BURNS AND THE RIGHT ROCK

(archival)

> *Now I lay me down to sleep*
> *I pray the Lord this bus to keep*

Routing is really out of this world on this stretch. We're boomeranging around California, sproing! up to Vancouver, back to Oregon, stop four hours from Portland to do a radio show, then we're off, flying up and down the California coast, then up and out to Minnesota, Ohio, Indiana, Nashville, Atlanta, and down to the South Carolina coast.

We have to be in Minneapolis on October 18, but we are being slowed by Bill's quest for stones. They are for a Walkway of the States he wants at his farmhouse, featuring a stone from every state. It seems we are leaving no stone unturned. On the morning of October 17 we are in Cheyenne at 8:30 a.m. By 3:30 p.m. we have stopped three times, once for a Wyoming rock, once for lunch at 11:00 a.m., a little while later at a rest area to look for a Nebraska rock. We finally reach Council Bluffs, Iowa, and suffer another setback: having failed to find a Nebraska rock, Bill orders the bus turned around. We head back across the Platte River, and by God, we do pick up a Nebraska rock.

This project makes me a little more happy to be crossing familiar ground, as each new territory represents a search for "a good rock from this state." And not just any rock. Trying to get ahead of the game, Franz got a California rock early on. But it wouldn't do. "I want a big rock, real long like the state," said Bill.

Some interesting conversations result. Our Silver Eagle is perched on the shoulder, while Bill scurries around on a wash or down an embankment. Truck drivers, many of them fans, see Bill Monroe's bus and hail us on the CB.

"Hey there, Bill MON-roe, do you need help? Are y'all OK?"

"We're alright," Franz answers. "We're looking for a rock."

In Ames, Iowa, the idea of pulling up short and getting rooms for the night is rejected. Our ETA in Minneapolis is still 4:00 a.m. We'll pull in somewhere around the Cities and wait through checkout time before getting a room, hopefully in early afternoon, after a 2,100-mile, fifty-one-hour ride (barring further delay).

Actually, if you count it this way, the trip is even longer: We started in Berkeley, California, about midnight on October 13. Rode to La Jolla, near San Diego, then back north to San Jose, from whence we sought rocks from every state across the American West to Minnesota. So, it's been five days since we've had a room, and three days since a shower, on the front end of what will be a 200-hour, 4,200-mile trip home. This is counting stage and downtime—all part of the journey.

Given mileage and time, I can compute our rate of travel: twenty miles per hour to Nashville from San Francisco via San Diego, San Jose, Minneapolis, Chicago, Cleveland, and Indianapolis.

How do we do it? Easy, like pulling teeth.

For example, on the south side of Milwaukee, bound for Chicago, I ask Bill for the location of the job. "Why, it's in Evanston." Where in Evanston? I ask. Exasperated, he says, "Let me check," and goes to his room to get the contract (which probably has a damn set of directions attached). "Levy Center in Evanston," he says. Where is Levy Center? "On Maple Street," he says. Do you have a street number? "Huh-uh."

So, we fart around in Evanston for about forty-five minutes, most of which is spent trying to find a way to get our twelve-foot, six-inch Silver Eagle bus under three rail overpasses with clearances that range from twelve feet, three inches, to twelve feet, ten inches, depending on the cross street. We're past two of them and looking for a way under or over the third when we hear from the back, "1700 Maple."

So, now that we've fucked away nearly an hour, Bill parts with the needed information. Typical.

We finally find Levy Center, and while we're parking the bus, Bill says, "We need to leave for these shows on time." This from the man who earlier in the day spent two hours dawdling at a truck stop in Wisconsin, and the rest of it hoarding the very information we needed to arrive at all.

But who's counting?

I am. For a tour beginning October 26 and ending November 21: twenty-seven days, sixteen gigs, thirteen thousand miles, nineteen states, and one Canadian province. Culinary highlights: huevos rancheros with green chili in Albuquerque, an honest-to-God filet mignon sandwich for $5.95 somewhere in Wyoming, baked spaghetti with white clam sauce in Chicago.

It's good to find bargains because I will come away from this tour with about $800 for the month.

Having followed us into a truck stop, a woman accosts Monroe: "Your bus stinks!"

"That must have been your feet," Bill says.

"Well! I thought you were a southern gentleman!" she replies.

"I am. That's why I'm telling you the truth," Bill says.

I look at my notes after a trip like this and think I should have more, but I don't. I've spent so much time trying *not* to think that it's affected my output. Like working in a mill with a clock in plain view, where time goes faster if you don't watch it, the touring goes more easily if you don't examine it too closely.

Oh! to lie in a bunk at the back of the bus, a few inches away from the rear wheels and across the aisle from a partially functional toilet, the piss-laden aroma only partially masked by diesel fumes, socks, underwear, and Franz's positively astounding foot odor—he used *my* bunk tonight, but we're talking about feet you can smell from the *front* of the bus. Add some remnants of pickled vegetables, empty tins of Vienna sausages, cigarette butts, and various spoiling foodstuffs in the wastebaskets, and voila! Bus bouquet!

And if I die before I wake
I pray the Lord this bus to take

39 RICH COMES ALONG FOR THE RIDE

(recollected)

At a time when I had few acquaintances in Nashville, and fewer friends, a visit from my buddy Rich Ziven was a welcome dose of normalcy. We had known each other from high school and become bandmates, and he was the best man at my wedding. In the surreal world I had entered, it was good to have someone around to share a laugh. And he knew Bill's music as well or better than I did, so we had that to talk about.

The Blue Grass Boys had a show in Galax, Virginia, at the end of the week. It was a short run: a six-hour ride, shows on Friday and Saturday, and return on Sunday. So I decided to see whether Rich could come along. I drove us to the Monroe Enterprises lot, figuring if Monroe said no Rich could just take the car back to my house and I'd get a ride back when we returned.

I had not asked Bill for such a favor before, so I was relieved that he was agreeable. I guess maybe he knew I was short on friends just then. I motioned for Rich to come on, and he was thrilled to board the *Blue Grass Special*.

As we rolled toward Virginia, we got up a game of poker. As usual, Baker was the master of ceremonies, providing a narrative for the proceedings. Rich was amused by Kenny's lingo. He had a nickname for each card: *deuce, trey, four spot, pop bottles*—he paused at six and asked Rich what he thought that was called. Rich shrugged. Kenny said, "That's a six, dammit!" Then *sevina, frog eyes, niner, tension, Johnny Boy, ladies, bossman,* and *sharp top*.

When we arrived, Monroe said he would put Rich and me in a room, but I'd have to go half on it. Sure, sure, I figured I'd buy it, I said, but Bill said no, that'll be fine. Rich and I headed to the motel restaurant for supper and wound up sitting with him. Bill was amenable, downright sociable and engaging (rare with him). Rich asked what his favorite food was. "Fried potatoes!" he said, "man, I love fried potatoes done right." He asked Rich what food he liked best. "Baked chicken, I guess," he said. Bill agreed that was awful good if it was done right, but there was some sorry chicken, too. Yeah, it's gotta be right, Rich agreed.

Later Rich said he was actually thinking of moussaka, but he thought chicken might be more of a bluegrass thing.

That night we played nearby at the Moose Lodge, where an eponymous trophy dominated the vertical space downstage. I'd have to be careful not to snag Bullwinkle with the scroll of the bass. "Reckon how fast he was going when he hit that wall?" Wayne mused.

The big show was Saturday night at the Ruritan Club. This was the wellspring of old-time mountain music: in the Blue Ridge, at Galax, sharing the show with the legendary old-time fiddler Tommy Jarrell. It couldn't be any more core than that. The music that night *was* the core.

Tommy's band opened the concert. Then, after Monroe's set, people cleared the floor and stacked the chairs, and Tommy played the dance. The crowd hooted and clapped as Bill led the way onto the floor—the old guy was quite a hoofer, and he had no trouble finding plenty of partners.

But what is unforgettable is the way Tommy wove his magic. "Trance" may be a new age genre, but the term is apt for what Tommy's fiddling conjured. The refrains grew hypnotic, a hush came over the hall, and the ancient Virginia reel was summoned. The dancers circled the floor, their steps melding with the music, their feet shuffling in unison and perfect time, the fiddle leading them—Tommy Jarrell, mountain medium, channeling music that started its journey west from Babylon centuries before.

And Tommy was funny as hell, too. After the show, back at the motel, he and Kenny cracked wise as they shared a mason jar and traded fiddle tunes. "This was one my daddy used to play," one would say, or, "I heard this one a long time ago, I can't remember where," and the other might say, "That puts me in the mind of," and pull one out that had a similar turn. Tommy played one he said his grandfather heard from a Confederate soldier, if the story was true.

They went that way until about three in the morning, when Tommy's daughter finally pulled the plug. Tommy said he wasn't tired, but his daughter prevailed.

I voted with Tommy. I hated to see them quit. And my friend Rich got one hell of a ride to Virginia that weekend.

40 THE POKER TO END ALL POKER

(partly archival)

"I think I shall smoke!" Baker would say, pulling out a Lucky with a flourish, lighting it, then holding it daintily with his fingertips, pinky extended, before dealing.

He must have played cards a lot in the navy. That's when he would most often speak of his time in the Pacific in World War II. His narration was certainly that of a sailor, delivered with all the proper modifiers and intensi-fiers.

Once Monroe took exception to the language being used in the presence of a (his) lady. We took our admonishment without argument. But I think Bill came to wish he hadn't said anything at all.

The next time we played in his presence, we laid it on pretty thick.

"Baker, pass me the blessed cards," Wayne said.

"Why, certainly!" Baker replied.

"Shall I deal them?" Wayne asked.

"Oh, yes, please do," I said.

I glanced at my hand. "My stars and garters! Please give me four," I said, then viewed my hand again. "Well, drat!"

Monroe rose from his seat, glared at us, and then went to his cabin amidships and slammed the door.

Before his surgery and reckoning with mortality, when repentance re-quired giving up the vice of gambling, Bill Monroe was the world's greatest poker player—the great American stone face. Lester Flatt loved poker, too, but Bill liked to brag about beating him and would say what a poor sport he was.

I know when I played Monroe I always lost—except once.

It was five-card stud, and I had just drawn two pairs. The other fellas had folded, and Monroe was the only one left. I glanced up at him.

Baker laughed out loud. "Son, you won't find nothin' there!" he said.

Even if you never met Bill, you can look at pictures of him and imagine that's where the expression *poker face* came from. He could be holding four queens or a busted straight, and you'd get the same impression of his face—a one-man Mount Rushmore.

Actually, on this hand Bill *was* holding four queens, probably from early on. Baker and Wayne, sensing trouble, had bowed out. I, having no sense, asked for more cards and drew a royal flush in spades.

Bill raised me. I raised him back. Bill doubled me. I doubled him back. Now Baker and Wayne were interested again. Bill began to sputter, "You're just playin' stupid, you don't know what you're doin'!" Probably blushing, I told him I thought I did. He saw my raise and spread out his queens to show me the error of my ways.

I spread out my royal flush. "Oh goddam!" Baker exclaimed under his breath and retreated to the back of the bus. Bill glared at me, and I thought for a moment either he or (more probably) I would go through the window. Big Mon did not like to lose.

That ended the game. Back at the bunks, Baker and Wayne were still chortling. If you're smart, Baker advised, don't ever mention it again. Ever.

41   BILL ON DOLLY, WAYNE ON BILL

(archival)

As we rolled out of Wilkesboro, North Carolina, on a snowy morning, Wayne and I were sitting up front in the bus playing gin and shooting the bull. Dolly Parton came on the radio singing "9 to 5," and we began talking about what a great musician she is, and a consummate pro to boot.

Monroe entered with, "She sure has got a filthy mouth on her. You never heard such filth as in that movie, boy . . . When a woman goes to usin' that filthy stuff, why, that ain't no lady."

"Well, I don't hold with using rough language onstage," Wayne countered. "But Dolly sure is a talent. Now, buddy, she is flat knocking it down."

Discussion ensued, and Bill's closer was, "Well, if it's written out for her, what words to say in the movie, then she's got to say them." Yeah, we agreed, that's right. Bill admitted, "Why, she's a big star on account of she's sellin' to the people."

Back in the bunks, Wayne savored holding his ground and letting Monroe defeat his own argument.

Wayne could get away with saying stuff to Bill no one else would. When we sidemen of the American Federation of Musicians, Nashville local 257 (of which band leaders are also members), attended a meeting about working conditions for sidemen and road musicians, we found we had a quorum. So we voted ourselves a nearly 100 percent raise, $110 per day plus a per diem. At the time, union scale was $60 per day on the days you had a show, and nothing on the days you weren't working—even if you were still on the road.

Bill wasn't happy. But when he said something about it, Wayne met him squarely.

"You could have voted, too," Wayne said. "I didn't see you there."

To his credit, Monroe took it like a man. And that was the last he spoke of it.

After this evening's show, we are in an empty pavilion at Lakeside Park in Roanoke, Virginia. The bus won't start—again. We had a lot of trouble with it last week, and Bill shelled out $1,800 to give it a general rundown, so tonight he is exasperated.

Nevertheless, Wayne is needling him. As Monroe and Baker are walking off to find something to eat while we wait for a mechanic, Wayne lobs a parting shot. "Hurry back now, so you can pay the man!"

Bill angled his head back at Wayne. His lips parted, one eyebrow shot up, and then, just when it looked like he was going to blow, the corners of his mouth turned up slightly. He turned back around and walked off, shaking his head.

Wayne slides by again.

WINNING IN TAHOE 42

(archival)

Here's how Bill does Caesars in Tahoe:

We fly into Reno, ride in a Lincoln limo to the hotel, unload our stuff, and stack it in the lobby. Then Bill Monroe, whose name is up in lights on the marquee out front, stands in line for a half hour waiting to check in.

Seems rooms are not included in the deal. Monroe pays $84 per room for three singles. He takes one, Kenny and Wayne take another, and Butch and I take the third—which turns out to be a love nest with a big jacuzzi and one bed. I win the flip, so Butch sleeps on the couch.

I thought, as is often the case on this type of gig, that we'd have a deal on meals. No deal. I have $40 on me for the next three days. We Boys probably have about $150 between the four of us.

And here I had been toying with the idea of gambling a little.

Our show in the Cascade Room goes well enough, all things considered. Wayne has the flu, at one point in the first set stepping out to chuck lunch backstage. Kenny has an abscessed tooth, swelling his cheek like a chaw of tobacco. By the second night, Butch has the flu (he also leaves the stage for a couple of tunes). I have bronchitis, which improves my bass singing.

Nonetheless, management seems pleased. Yet, in addition to having to pay for rooms, Monroe is charged $40 for dressing room refreshments.

But the kicker comes at the airport on the way out. Checking in for our flight home, we find Monroe is the only one holding a confirmed ticket. The rest of us are on standby—and this is Sunday on New Year's weekend. And, yes, we get stuck in Dallas.

I come here not to praise Caesars.

43 MONROE PAYS THE PIPER

(archival)

Monroe feels that anything more than twenty-five dollars for a motel room is exorbitant. Consequently, we find ourselves in some strange places.

Our room at the Sandman motel in Bristol, Virginia, is mostly yellow. Gold doorknobs, red-and-green floral drapes, nonmatching yellow bedspreads. There are palm prints on the ceiling and fluorescent tubes over the plywood headboards.

Franz is pacing the room. He wants the corpulent desk clerk to come over and run her hands through his Vitalis. Monroe and Baker have gone out to look the town over and do some shopping. I might have gone, but I'm not up for an afternoon of sparring with those two.

Instead, I've snuck my fun in (blowing it out the bathroom window), so I'm content to lay back, watch daytime TV, and listen to the trucks roll out of the hills toward I-81 on the Lee Highway. The man on the soap opera drinks too much, and his weird wife is annoyed by this. He's bummed, too. "Why haven't we made love since my resignation?" he asks.

I don't blame him. I'd have a drink, too, on such a winter's day in Bristol at the Sandman.

Another time in Bristol—but this time Bristol, *Tennessee*—we stayed at one more of these gems. It was colder in the room than it was outside (with no extra blankets), and you had to run around in the shower to get wet. Our rooms heated up eventually, except for Monroe's.

The next morning we were all on the bus waiting for him when he came on and asked Franz whether he had a wrench. Franz nodded and asked what it was for. "I need to fix the toilet, it's fallen apart," Bill replied. Franz got a wrench and headed for the back of the bus, but Bill said, "No, it's in my room."

I went with Franz to see. The whole commode had tipped over. (Don't know if it was with or without Bill.) Franz pondered it for a minute and said, "Well, hell, let's just go."

The next day I bought a *National Lampoon* magazine, and in the True Facts column I found an item about a woman who was suing Knox County and the City of Knoxville for $25,000. It seems a wall-mounted toilet had collapsed with her on it. According to the suit, she "now suffers from a fear of toilets . . . and is forced to search for toilets securely attached to the floor."

What is it with East Tennessee? When I showed this to Monroe, he read it, moving his lips soundlessly, then stared straight ahead.

Oh well. I thought it was humorous. Wayne and Franz cackled for me.

THE FIRST THING I'M GOING TO DO 44

(archival)
At the end of a monthlong tour, we find out that we're going to spend one night in Nashville before we take care of the rest of the dates we have this week out east. We'll be home three days sooner than we expected. This is good news to all of us, and talk turns to what we'll do when we get there.

Says Monroe, who's feeling sick (sinuses), sore (back), and old: "I'm gonna go out in the woods with some blankets, plenty of blankets, and I'll find me a nice, quiet spot a'way on out there, boy, and I'm gonna get down in a place and pull all the blankets over me and just not move a'tall . . ."

Wayne says, "I called Sue and told her to have me a hill o' beans with some raw onions and buttermilk and green 'maters and cornbread . . ."

Kenny says, "I'm going straight to a damn restaurant and have me about six different kinds of vegetables set out in front of me . . ."

Butch, who lives in Virginia, says, "Shit, man, I ain't goin' home for a while. I'm gonna *sleep* . . ."

Me? To paraphrase Baker on another such occasion, I am going to pet the dog, make love to my wife, and then set my bags down.

45 BEAN BLOSSOM INTERNATIONAL

(recollected)

Bill was proud of the international audience that traveled to Bean Blossom. The figure I often heard was that thirty different countries were represented there in Indiana.

It was an unscientific count, and probably should have included a margin of error. I heard about a woman who approached Joe Val to tell him how much she enjoyed his show. She asked where he was from, and Joe said New England. She asked how he liked it in our country.

There was no mistaking the large contingent from Japan. They're great bluegrass fans, and they went everywhere together, in groups of ten, twenty, or more, toting cameras and instruments, and leaving tea samples and origami all over the park.

And they picked like the dickens! Late one night, mandolin player Mike Compton stepped away from a crowded jam session to search for a smaller group. He was back in five minutes. I asked where he'd been. He said he was out in the woods and nearly got run over by a Japanese ensemble marching through the dark, playing like hell.

Bill liked to invite the foreign visitors onstage to play, too, and various European players cherished the moment, such as the Kruger brothers, teens from Switzerland. There were fifteen or twenty Japanese players, so many that they set up a rotation—four or five of them would emerge from the door on stage right, while four or five would make room and leave by the door on stage left. I was standing backstage when they fired off into Monroe's instrumental "Rawhide" at a ridiculous tempo.

"My God, that's fast!" I said to the interpreter.

"Thank you!" he said, bowing.

Out in a field adjacent to the Amen Corner, there was a wild group of Canadians flying the Maple Leaf from their motor home, which was ringed by cases of Labatt beer stacked several high. They were pickers, too. One of them, wearing a floppy bush hat and shoulder-length locks, played a toaster, making a sound like a washboard.

He came to the record table to tell me, "I asked Bill could I come up and jam, and he said noooo, it's electric, eh?"

One afternoon, Ailene Peva, perennially one of the festival's most gracious hostesses, brought a tall, skinny Italian guy to the record table and introduced him to me. This was Savino: He played great guitar but didn't speak much English. Did I know anyone who spoke French, maybe?

I was game. "Parlez-vous français?" I asked, nearly exhausting my vocabulary.

"Oh, oui!" he said, before rattling off a paragraph I never understood.

"Whoa, I don't! I was just wondering if you do," I said, before explaining I could speak "un petit peu," using the hand gesture I learned in high school to indicate yes, I am a stupid American.

After a few of my halting attempts at French charades, Savino said, "Maybe English is better."

Eventually, he told me he was in the States for a few weeks and would be visiting Nashville after Bean Blossom was over. I gave him my phone number and invited him to give me a call when he was in town.

The following week he did call. "It ees Savino," he said.

"Savino! Are you in Nashville? Where are you staying?"

"The Bell Motel," he said, accenting his *l*'s. Wary of his surroundings, he had left there and gone downtown. The hotels there looked bad, too.

"Where are you now?"

"At ze corner of Third and Broad Way."

"Third and Broadway? Oh, Savino, you've got to get out of there!"

"Yes," he said. "Ze people here are not good. Zey are stealers."

I agreed. I told him to wait there and I would come pick him up. After bringing him back to East Nashville, I decided I would need to enlist an interpreter. Lionel Wendling, a French musician who lived fifteen minutes away in Madison, was just the man for the job. Furthermore, he was willing to put him up.

Finally we began to learn about Savino, who could play like the wind but was nearly as groundless. Sixteenth notes flowed like vino, but rhythm was not his forte. He was new to the music.

We went to visit Jerry Douglas, whose teenage sister-in-law was visiting and instantly developed a crush on the soft-spoken, wide-eyed Italian. ("He's *cute!*" she whispered to us in the kitchen.) She asked whether he liked to play cards, and he said yes, sometimes, but he didn't know what games he could play. "Oh, I'll teach you," she said, dealt out poker hands, and began to explain. Soon, Savino held up his hand and nodded to indicate he understood.

Then he turned over a full house. "Zees game I know, I think," he said.

46 ALL DAY AT THE RECORD TABLE

(partly archival)

The respective roles of the Blue Grass Boys were well settled by the decade I came along. The guitar player sang lead on the trios, the banjo player sang baritone, the bass player sang bass, and Baker would be the Greatest Fiddle Player in Bluegrass Music.

Offstage and at home, certain of the Boys might go out to Bill's farm and help out around the place, fixing a gate, planting fence posts, or what have you. But I found that stories of the Boys being pressed into duty working the farm or tending the festival grounds were either exaggerated or outdated.

Having been raised in a city of sixty thousand, I was ignorant of farm life. But having heard some of the conversation, I found it easy to beg off when the Boys would kid me about not helping out around Bill's place. "Oh, I don't know," I would say, "I don't think you'd want me around. I'd go off and leave the wrong gate open or close the wrong gate or scare the horses or something."

One night at Bean Blossom, after the last show of the year, Bill had a lowboy trailer with a few cows delivered to the grounds. I was still hanging around—the bus wasn't going to leave until Monroe was ready to go—and Bill called me over to give him a hand.

"Now, just stand right over there," he directed. Then he let down the gate on the trailer. "Now call 'em," he said.

"Call 'em? What do I call them?" I asked. Bill looked at me like, *You stupid thang. Don't you know nothin'?*

"Just call 'em!" he said. Then, seeing it was hopeless, he came around to where I was and called the cattle. "C'mon, Bossie, c'mon now," a low whistle, "here now," and the cattle began filing toward us.

I did better at the record table (again, traditionally the bass player's job). Bill had more than twenty titles in print at the time. I stored stock under the bus, and from there I filled a couple of boxes of records and cassettes to carry to the merchandise table, along with perhaps some black-and-white glossy prints or other souvenir items. On a fair day I might sell a dozen albums and maybe a half-dozen cassettes—seven dollars for an album, eight dollars for a cassette, ten dollars for the *Bean Blossom* live double album. Bill would pay me about 10 percent of the take, so I took it seriously and did my best.

But it did make for a long day. If it was a well-attended show, I needed to be out there as soon as we hit the grounds and stay as long as there were people around. I met a lot of great people, but I put up with even more people than that. A fairly typical sale might go like this:

Customer looks over a tableful of albums, looks at me, and asks, "How much?"

"Single albums are seven dollars; tapes are eight; the double albums are ten. We have tapes of all the albums you see here on the table."

Customer picks up a single album. "How much for this 'un?"

"Seven dollars."

"Do you have a tape of this?"

"Yessir, we do." I pick up a cassette and hand it to him.

"How much?"

"Eight dollars." My blood pressure rises slightly.

"I bought a tape from y'all two years ago at Bean Blossom."

I nod. "I've not been with Bill that long."

"I didn't play it but once, and it broke." He eyes me suspiciously.

I am imagining him at home with a GE Loudmouth player and a pile of dusty eight-tracks beside it. "Well, sometimes a machine can do that to a tape, too."

"Eight dollars, you say?"

"Yessir."

"Do you have tapes of these others?"

And so on. After we spent a week at the Missouri State Fair, Blake remarked that the reason they call it the Show-Me State is "because you can't tell them people nothin'."

My dad said when people are at leisure they are not thinking. They might be reasonably intelligent at work, but when they're off the clock they turn off their brains.

And there was another factor I had failed to consider at all.

We had gone from Gettysburg, Pennsylvania, where if anything people asked too many questions, to Yanceyville, North Carolina, where they asked questions you could answer by repeating what you had just said. At the record table, they ran their fingers over the album covers, trying to comprehend the liner notes. One woman holding an album asked me how many songs were on it. I counted them for her. A man looking at a box of cassette tapes with their titles facing up asked me whether they were all different.

Afterward, back on the bus, I was marveling at all of this, and Wayne gently said, "Son, they couldn't read."

It honestly hadn't occurred to me. I learned to look more closely at the fans who came to the table—like in Warren, Michigan, a city that was a shell of its former auto-manufacturing community. There, an enthusiastic crowd gathered around the table, many of them transplanted southerners who had moved north to take good factory jobs. Now everything was boarded up. They would have bought a lot of records—but they couldn't afford them. I had a lot of happy conversations, but no sales.

Sideman or not, I could never complain much about the fan interface. No fans, no job. Engaging the audience is what professionals are expected to do, at least in bluegrass music. Rock and rollers may hide behind a stage pass and an attitude, but that is not the way in bluegrass, not even for the stars. If Bill Monroe could give any and all fans some of his time, I damn sure could.

But even Bill had his limit. Describing someone who had been excep-
tionally boring or annoying, he'd say, "Sht! That man liked to worry me to
death!"

BLUEGRASS DEATH TRIP 47

(recollected)

The hardest thing about working the record table was the long, long hours,
all day and all night. I might get a little relief from one of the Boys, but it
was mainly up to me to sit there the whole time.

This gave me the chance to hear every set that every band at the festival
played. Depending on the festival and the bands, it could be a *really* long day.
In twelve- and fourteen-hour days, I spent the time yakking with friends
and fans, drinking a lot of coffee, and listening to a lot of music—most of
it not great, forming the mean on which "above average" is based.

I devised other ways to pass the time, such as analyzing and grouping
oft-repeated lyrical themes. They call it the "high, lonesome sound," but you
could just call it mournful. Sorrow and death run deep in country music,
and the old-time stuff is especially dark.

These songs are of a time not so long ago, especially in Appalachia, when
not all the children survived, and people died young of disease, war, or awful
wrecks. The most morbid and maudlin songs seem to be the most popular,
and from early on supply has chased demand.

There are the disaster songs, like "Wreck of the Old 97," or "Down with
the Old Canoe" (about the *Titanic*). For children and parents, there are
"Little Rosewood Casket," "The Little Girl and the Dreadful Snake," or "Put
My Little Shoes Away," to name only three. There are more for the parents
and grown children, such as "The Letter Edged in Black," "Will the Circle
Be Unbroken," "Memories of Mother and Dad," and "Mother's Not Dead
(She's Only Sleeping)."

Old-time music is especially tough on women, as in "Pretty Polly" (she
gets stabbed) and "Banks of the Ohio" (she is drowned), though variety is

provided by songs like "Secret of the Waterfall" (the woman *and* the man die at the hands of a jealous lover) and "Philadelphia Lawyer," set in Reno, Nevada, where a cowboy dispatches the city slicker romancing his wife (country folks gotta like that). "The Long Black Veil" is in a subset of songs where brave men die to preserve a woman's honor. There are even farewell songs to beloved animals, like "Old Blue" (dog) and "Goodbye Old Pal" (which posits that you can't beat a dead horse). And this is to say nothing of the universal carnage in "This World Is Not My Home" or "He Will Set Your Fields on Fire."

But even songs without death as a central theme will mention it anyway. One summer, perhaps goaded by another screeching rendition of "How Great Thou Art," I started keeping track of just how morbid the lyrics are.

My method was primitive but sufficiently accurate. Making hash marks on the lid of a record box, I kept two columns of tallies: one for every song I heard, and another for every song in which death was mentioned either directly or indirectly. The song didn't have to be about death, only mention it. Say the words, get a hash mark:

> "But the guilty one, now she lies dying." *Bing!*
> "When I die, won't you bury me on the mountain." *Bing!*
> "My mother and dad are laid there to rest." *Bing!*
> "Now she's up in heaven, she's with the angel band." *Bing!*
> "We'll meet in Heaven someday." *Bing!*

The results: in more than 80 percent of the songs, somebody is going to die, dies, or has died. Many of these songs are upbeat numbers, but nearly all of them have feet in the here and the after.

48 BILL KEEPS GRINDING

(archival, with a foreword from February 20, 1982)
Made another trip to Galax, Virginia, to play a dance at the Ruritan Club, where fiddler Tommy Jarrell's old-time band opens the show, then plays the dance after. Folks pull the folding chairs off the concrete floor and throw some green slickum down, Tommy starts in, and everyone dances.

Monroe likes these dances, and we always stay after to make a few rounds. But tonight, unlike the last time, Bill looked old on the dance floor. Normally light on his feet, he shuffled around the floor a few times and was spent. After he left the room and was out of public sight, his shoulders slumped and he seemed to shrink.

As I stood watching him go, a man came up and asked, "Y'all comin' back this way next year?" It caught me broadside. I realized what a good question that was. "I hope so," I replied.

February 26 and 27, 1982: Graham, North Carolina, Friday night; Statesville, North Carolina, on Saturday

Execution (or the natural way of it): Leave the lot at Monroe Enterprises on Friday at 2 a.m. Immediately go to the "Keys" (a truck stop on Trinity Lane) to fuel and eat, then head for Graham, North Carolina, arriving at 2 p.m. Inexpensive (albeit seedy) lodging readily available, but we park on the street for three hours. Then we get lost trying to find a cafeteria three blocks away.

After supper we arrive at the Big O Jamboree at six for a show at eight. The band is crabby. It's a loud, dumb, hateful set we play that night.

After the show, with a snowstorm brewing, we depart for Statesville (ninety-five miles away). Now, we could stay in town at the aforementioned cheap motel with an adjoining eatery, be in the rooms by 1:30 a.m., and depart the next day.

But no. We follow a car with A. L. Wood and Wayne Lewis looking for a place to eat, then on to Statesville. The highway is already getting slick. Monroe, dissatisfied with the progress of the restaurant search, orders the driver to drop off the Wood/Lewis lead car and instead exit for a truck stop with a sign outside that says "Diesel/No Food." We get back on the highway and continue toward Statesville. Exit again for a pancake house. It's closed. Back on the interstate, it's 3:15 a.m., road conditions worsening, and the driver's side windshield wiper, loaded with freezing slush, begins to malfunction. I hear our driver, Charlie Whitaker, say, "Ah, ah, there she goes!" as the wiper finally fouls, one inch of blade touching the glass, the remainder ice encrusted and flailing uselessly as our Silver Eagle skates through the North Carolina hills.

Charlie starts looking for a place to park for the night. I return to my bunk to finish James Kirkwood's *P.S. Your Cat Is Dead.*

Jefferson City, Tennessee

Monroe has Charlie cruising the town for an hour looking for the barber shop where he got his hair cut the last time he was in Jefferson City (God knows when that was). Charlie hasn't slept more than four hours at a time in the last four days, but he keeps smiling.

Around 3 A.M., in some little roadhouse in Eastern Kentucky, near Salyersville

Blake, Charlie, and I were having a bite and listening to the jukebox. "I Just Think I'll Go Away" came on with Carter Stanley singing the lead, and Charlie and I compared goosebumps.

"Oh, Lord!" Charlie said in his deep bass voice, "That tore me down." He handed Blake a quarter and said, "Go ahead and play that again, son, I've got to hear that one more time."

Blake got up and walked over to the jukebox. As he was looking up the tune, Monroe walked into the diner. Preempting a tirade on the inferiority of the Stanley Brothers, Blake pocketed the quarter and returned to the table.

Charlie looked up from his hotcakes and said, "J'ye play it?" Blake glanced toward Monroe, smiled, and said no. Matter-of-factly, around a mouthful of 'cakes, Charlie drawled, "I ought to kill you," and dug into another forkful.

Charlie was an eloquent, self-made man. He built a scrap-metal business up in Kentucky, sold it off for a fortune, and lived the good life in southern Ohio, running a bus and performing with his wife in their band, Lillie Mae and the Dixie Gospelaires. He drove Monroe's bus at his leisure. He didn't need the money.

Behind Charlie's deep, slow, southern drawl and unflappable disposition was a keen intellect and unassailable common sense. Late one night, I was riding shotgun and telling him it was good to get back on the road. We were paid by the day, and the calendar had been a little bare lately. Money was tight.

"Waal," he said, "if you get in a bad fix here's what you do. Write up all your checks for all your bills. Then put 'em all in the wrong envelopes. Send your 'lectric to the phone company, your phone to the gas company, and like that. Then wait for them all to call, apologize, and promise to write them another check right away. That'll get you two or three weeks until everything gets straightened out. By then you've got the money, just make new checks for everybody."

No wonder he was already retired.

Easter weekend at Bean Blossom

Left Nashville at 2 a.m. on Saturday, arriving at Bean Blossom at 9 a.m. It will be a sparsely attended show starting at two or three this afternoon (or maybe later), but, by God, we're here. Bill likes to come here and sit. Sometimes we'll be rolling along on I-65 in Indiana, and we'll make the thirty-mile detour just to come here and look at the place.

Today it's cold in the early spring, and the potbelly stoves in the Brown County Jamboree music barn are fired up, pouring as much smoke as heat into the place.

Shorty Hancock, one of Bill's farmhands, is up from Tennessee. He's a stout man with a crew cut and a gravelly alto voice usually heard delivering some insufficient explanation to a demand from Bill. I think the Boss keeps him handy to have someone to berate.

When Bill sees flames jumping out the top on one of the stoves, he hollers for Shorty, who waddles the length of the barn as quickly as he can to answer the panic.

That's business more or less as usual here. But now, with Bill's brother Birch, the park's longtime caretaker, in failing health, it's more ramshackle than ever. I had to walk down the road to use someone's outhouse. Nothing functional here.

There is a stage at one end of the music barn, and a backstage room behind that with another potbelly stove. I was outside at that end of the building when the door flew open and Blake came staggering out, coughing and doubling over in laughter. I looked at him, and all he could do was point at the chimney. Thick, white smoke was pouring out from the cap, the flue, the flashing, even the eaves.

Once Blake stopped convulsing, he told me the story. Monroe had come into the back room and found the stove going cold. He hollered for Shorty, who came in, took a look, and went back out again. Directly, he returned with a tin cup of kerosene.

The rest transpired before Bill could finish yelling at him. Shorty opened the top of the stove and dumped the kerosene into it, and the room filled with smoke. Bill was saying, "Now, Shorty, what do you think that's gonna do?" when Shorty pulled out a match and—as Bill yelled, "No, Shorty!"— struck the match and threw it into the stove. Flame leaped out of the top and from all the vents. Bill shouted, "Damn, Shorty, you're gonna kill us all!" and Blake busted out of the back door, laughing so hard he had to sit and catch his breath before he could explain.

Bill's account was more succinct. "That Shorty ain't got a lick o' sense, man, he liked to kill us all, I ain't kiddin'!"

Hannibal, Missouri

We needed to get up here early so Bill could see some cattle. It's an eight-hour trip from Nashville, so we needed to leave at 2 a.m. That's OK—all I would do at home is sleep.

I pulled into the Monroe Enterprises lot, ready to go, at 1:45 a.m. No bus. I drove to the nearby bus garage, and sure enough, there it sat, with Charlie trying to undo whatever repair had been wreaked on it earlier in the day. It was about 4 a.m. when he finally got the bus going so we could get started on our music/cattle excursion.

Carrying my luggage onto the bus, I noticed two wooden live-animal containers in the little lounge just forward of the bunks. Briefly speculating on their possible contents (without looking), I stowed my gear.

Just before dawn we stopped to eat, and I chewed my way through a breakfast of playful insults (this was the usual if Monroe thought any of the boys were feeling put out). Back on the bus, I crawled into my bunk and read a little as the sun was coming up. I switched off my light and laid back to sleep.

Just as I was dozing off, I heard the first one. Then both roosters started crowing.

49 CHECKING ON PAYCHECK

(recollected)

We played a big show at the Waikiki Shell in Honolulu with Terri Gibbs and Johnny Paycheck, but the routing left little time to enjoy a trip to Hawai'i. We had already pulled a couple of overnighters by the time we arrived at the Cincinnati airport to park for the night and fly out at dawn. It was a strange flight, leaving just before the sun rose and running away from it all day so it felt like a night trip.

Paycheck and his band were on the same flight, and if Paycheck was bothered by fatigue or the flight time it certainly did not show. He was feeling no pain. In fact, a flight attendant who had noticed that Wayne and Paycheck were acquainted (they both came from southern Ohio and had chatted before takeoff) came back from first class to ask Wayne whether he would mind coming up to keep company with "Mr. Paycheck." She would open the 747's upper-level lounge for them. He was "bothering" some of the first-class passengers.

Wayne was just the man for the job. He and Paycheck spent a good part of the flight up in the lounge, where Wayne drank for free and Paycheck was so coked up he was spitting teeth out on the carpet. Wayne's mission was accomplished. He had occupied Paycheck, and when they ran out of steam, Wayne brought him back to coach, where his band and ours were sitting. Well sedated, they both went to sleep.

It was early afternoon in Honolulu when we landed. As the passengers rose from their seats, Monroe confronted Paycheck, who was just starting to come around.

"Johnny Paycheck!" he said.

Paycheck righted himself and looked up at Monroe. "Mr. Bill Monroe!" he replied.

Bill said, "Are we working this show together?"

"Yessir!" Paycheck replied.

"Are we gonna work hard?" Bill demanded.

"Yessir!"

"Are we gonna stand firm?"

Paycheck faltered, his mental processes not quite up to speed. Both bands fell out laughing.

We went straight from the airport to the concert venue for a sound check before going to the hotel to shower and shave. Julia LaBella was along on the trip; she told me that later that afternoon Monroe paid a visit to Paycheck's dressing room. He wanted to see that Paycheck would be able to hold up his part of the show.

Entering the dressing room, Monroe found Paycheck sitting there with his guitar, wearing a bandanna, sunglasses, and a red T-shirt with white Coca-Cola logotype that read "Cocaine."

Monroe leaned forward to peer at the shirt and then at Paycheck, and said, "Uh, what does that mean?"

Again, Paycheck was at a loss for an answer.

All the bands got through the show just fine, and then we had the better part of the next day to take in a little bit of Honolulu before flying out that night. Pressing my luck, I accepted an invitation to a luau by some fellas from Minnesota I met at the record table. We had a high time, but we were a little late getting to the airport, and I was considerably worse for the wear. I made the plane alright, but Bill wasn't happy.

50 MULE DAY, APRIL 3, 1982, COLUMBIA, TENNESSEE

(recollected)

Bill's love of horses and mules was well known and found frequently in his repertoire: There was "Muleskinner Blues," of course, along with "Molly and Tenbrooks" and "Goodbye Old Pal," plus instrumentals such as "Wheel Hoss" and "The Old Gray Mare Came Tearing Out of the Wilderness." He relished describing how to manage horses or a team of mules. Where other men his age might keep pictures of grandchildren, he had pictures of his mules. "Ain't she pretty?" he would ask, showing someone one of his pictures. He was often seen riding around the festival grounds at Bean Blossom in a wagon pulled by mules.

So, it was fitting that he presided as grand marshal of the Mule Day parade in Columbia, Tennessee. It looked like it would be fun on a windy but sunny day in early spring.

However, in practice it would be a little tough. Monroe and all his Blue Grass Boys would be aboard a wagon pulled by a team of mules. At the rear of the wagon was a painted plywood banner with Bill's name and title as grand marshal. At the front of the wagon was a pair of small speakers. As I eyed the setup, I thought I should stand at the rear. For one, onstage or in a parade, it's customary for the leader to be out front. Secondly, the plywood banner might be an airfoil as well as a backstop to lean on, as I was the only one in the band who had to stand up to play.

Bill felt differently. He thought he should be sitting under his name. As with any performance, I stood wherever Bill thought I should stand. So, I stood at the front of the wagon as Bill and the Boys took their seats.

All of them had enough farm experience to know better than I what would happen next.

It's important here to note that when mules "start," it doesn't mean they *begin*. Think of it as the root word of *startle*—the mules plunge forward, and not gently, to get the wagon rolling. When the driver called, "Up!" the mules started, the wagon lurched forward, and the bass and I went over backward, landing in Blake and Kenny's laps as Baker yelled, "Ho!" and everyone laughed.

I righted myself, tried a couple of different stances, and finally jammed my feet under one of the speakers that was lashed to the wagon. After that, when the mules started or my bass caught a gust of wind, I hung by my toes to stay upright. I finished the parade without going down again.

So, it was a fun day. And when a picture of us appeared in the Nashville paper the next morning, my neighbors, country folks from Missouri, were thrilled. Mules, Bill Monroe, and their own neighbor!

It may be the only photo ever taken with me at the front of the band.

OPENING THE KNOXVILLE WORLD'S FAIR, MAY 1, 1982   51

(archival)

After a Friday show in Thomasville, Georgia, we boarded a private jet to Knoxville, Tennessee, for the opening of the 1982 World's Fair, officially known as the Knoxville International Energy Exposition.

Bill was on the outs with the Boys that night. But there was a wet bar on the plane, so we dug in and helped ourselves. Bill's friend Julia LaBella was along for the ride and joined us for bourbon (we were happy to keep her glass full). When we got to the motel, she still wanted to party. With a nod toward Bill, who was already walking toward his room, she said, "He ain't gonna do nothing but go to sleep."

But there was no time for further foolishment. We had to be up at 6 a.m. to get to the park by 8 a.m. for shows at 11 a.m. and 4 p.m.

The reason for the early arrival was to account for the tightest presidential security we ever saw. Ronald Reagan would be delivering an opening address, and it was a little more than a year after John Hinckley Jr. had tried to assassinate him.

We played three times for Jimmy Carter while I was in the band, but security was never like this. First the Secret Service agents and Knox County troopers cordoned off the backstage area, climbing the surrounding hills, rooftops, trees, and any other high points. G-men in blue suits with burp guns under their wired jackets wouldn't let anyone back out once they were through the metal detectors and baggage and instrument checks (they stuck a flashlight up my bass). All of us—Blue Grass Boys, Boy Scouts, Girl Scouts, Cub Scouts, US Marines, dancers—were conducted to a secured, roped-off area one hundred yards from the stage, where we remained for hours.

There were no restrooms in the secured area, potentially leaving scores of Cub Scouts jiggling for hours. I pointed this out to a Secret Service agent, who spoke into his sleeve and got authorization to shift the rope twenty feet over to include the restrooms. (It was my patriotic contribution to the event.)

Then, a half hour before Reagan arrived, security packed everyone inside a tiny tourist information pavilion and closed the doors behind us (even the marines, those notorious prez-killers). Another wave of Secret Service, and then a K9 bomb squad. Dogs sniffing everywhere, Secret Service checking empty soda cans and coffee cups. Then another wave of county cops, six motorcycle cops, three county cruisers, two Secret Service limos, and a Ronald in a pear tree (the last and biggest limo). Mr. and Mrs. Reagan sat behind the stage in the idling limo for about five minutes, while the Secret Service combed the area *again*. Then, boom! Reagan was out of the limo and hustled to the stage to enter an eight-foot-tall bulletproof booth for a TV broadcast that would show his friendly, informal visit with the good people of Knoxville. On the screen you couldn't see he was enclosed in glass.

After his speech, boom! offstage, into the limo, zoom out of there with reporters dashing to their cars to catch up. We were not allowed out of the building until Reagan had finished his speech, scurried out to his limo, and sped away.

Then it was on with the show. Dinah Shore, a native Tennessean, emceed the extravaganza, which also featured two or three Up with People–type peppy song-and-dance groups along with Ricky Skaggs and Porter Wagoner.

We were all syncing to prerecorded music for the telecast. Obviously, the others had more experience at this and were more adept. When Bill was introduced, he walked over to a line of mikes that had been struck for the dancers and took his spot there, at right angles to the audience. I called out to him, "Might as well face the crowd! Those mikes are dead!" He was confused.

The recording was an older version of "Blue Moon of Kentucky" with two or three fiddles on the intro. Baker, not playing the game, stood there and waved his bow like a conductor, while Blake, Wayne, and I bobbed around trying to look like we were with Bill. And the dancers, who had never really gone away, stood around with big smiles and swayed appreciatively.

Of course, I didn't see the live broadcast. But it couldn't have looked good. As I said, we don't do a lot of sync performances. Afterward, Bill said, "The man on that record had a lot better voice."

UNCLE BIRCH AND SOUTHERN FUNERARY TRADITIONS 52

(archival)

Morbid lyrics in country songs are just one aspect of old-time southern funerary traditions. There's plenty more.

When Lester Flatt passed away, Monroe sent a floral arrangement featuring a blue plastic telephone and a card that said, "Jesus Called." (To which one wag appended, "But I took the gig!")

I experienced some of that old-time religion for myself at the funeral of Bill's brother Birch, who died on May 15, 1982. Services were held at a little white church in their hometown of Rosine, Kentucky. The Gospel Coalminers provided the appropriate musical melancholy.

After two preachers spoke at length, I watched in silent shock and dread as ushers removed the flowers and drapes from around the bier to open the casket. Lifting the corpse, they propped Birch up a tad, laid his hat on his chest, and placed his fiddle in the crook of his arm. We all filed by to pay our respects, and then past the family to offer condolences.

A year later, we returned to the cemetery for a memorial service and the unveiling of a sizable two-level gravestone. The epitaphs inscribed there read, "FIDDLER, FRIEND OF ALL" and "A WONDERFUL BROTHER, A WONDERFUL UNCLE." The primitive two-dimensional art etched above depicted a table on which rested a hat, a fiddle and bow, and a pair of glasses.

Overall, the monument looked like a 1960s artist's rendering of a futuristic drive-through bank. When it was unveiled, Blake and I didn't dare look at each other. As preposterous as it looked—it was the *glasses* that got me—that would be the worst time possible to get a case of the giggles. The solemnity of the occasion only made the tickle worse. After a few minutes at the graveside, Blake and I went back to my car. Both of us stared straight ahead, not speaking, as I eased down the hill to the highway. Only after I turned out of the drive and began to speed away did we turn and look at each other—and then burst out laughing till we cried.

No disrespect to Birch, none at all. But it was all too much. Southern funerals can take a lot out of you.

PART VII
"PRECIOUS MEMORIES"

(archival)

Given: Friday in Texas, Saturday off, and Sunday in Woodville, Alabama, at Cathedral Caverns. Monroe had to fly to DC to accept an award on Saturday, sans Blue Grass Boys. When we first discussed plans, Bill thought he might have to fly into Birmingham (three hours south of Woodville). Since Woodville is three hours south of Nashville, it would seem more logical to drop Monroe near the airport in Dallas–Fort Worth on the way out of Texas, head to Nashville, and pick him back up there to drive to Alabama.

But no. We come out of Oak Ridge Ranch, go to DFW, park for the night until Bill's flight takes off, go to breakfast, stop to get the bus washed (!), then take twenty-two hours dillydallying back to Scottsboro, Alabama, so we can meet Bill at Huntsville, Alabama (thirty miles from the festival and another fifteen from Scottsboro).

But what tops this is on the previous Thursday night, as we pull out of Nashville, I learn that we will be recording an album on Sunday. I wish I had the bass I record with, because this one's buzzing a little bit. Not a big deal for a live show, but not great for high-fidelity recording.

Monroe wanted to record in the Cathedral Caverns because he liked the massive echo in the cave. Later, I heard he had run into Pat Enright downtown in Nashville and described the album he wanted to do and the sound of the cave.

"Gee, Bill, that sounds pretty weird," Pat said.

"I hope so!" Monroe replied.

But no one ever told me about it. I knew about the upcoming date, but Monroe never mentioned anything about recording. So, when I told him that Georgia was expecting a baby in July, and that I wanted to be there for the birth if I could, Bill lined up a replacement. I didn't know about that either.

There were a lot of variables in my itinerary calculations. We were in a busy stretch that entailed some brutal routing. As Georgia's due date approached, we had shows scheduled in Texas, Alabama, North Carolina, and

Nova Scotia. Doing some advance work on airline reservations, I had a list of flight connections from Halifax that looked like hieroglyphics.

Monroe was making complex calculations, too. As we were pulling out of the show in Texas, Bill asked us what songs we thought would be good for the album. As it worked out, he chose only three songs we had ever performed before. And when he couldn't reach the bass singer he wanted to replace me, he went through the union and hired a second guy. But then the first guy got wind of it, and he showed up, too. Apparently, Monroe felt obligated to use them both. So one replaced me, and the other replaced Blake to sing the baritone part.

So now the gospel-singing Blue Grass Quartet had two new, temporary members who had never sung anything with the band. And though Cathedral Caverns offered a welcome coolness in July in Alabama, the damp air and the water dripping from the ceiling made it impossible to keep the instruments in tune. There were sheets of plastic everywhere.

The *coup de grâce* was delivered by Walter Haynes, the producer and audio engineer whose job had to be threatened before he consented to try this thing. It seemed his heart was still not in it, because he brought a remote recording outfit with an eight-channel board. Count with me, now—five instruments, four singers, eight channels.

Bill was right about the reverberation in the cave. It was powerful, alright—more than Haynes could handle, even if he had brought adequate equipment, which he did not.

In one more "fix it in the mix" promise, he said he would transfer it all to twenty-four track back at the studio. So, we would have a second-generation master before it went anywhere else. And imagine how well any studio overdubs might blend in with the cave sound.

The results were what you might expect—"a hash," as engineer Vic Gabany put it. (The album was never released, but parts of it are heard in the 2006 Bear Family CD collection *My Last Days on Earth*, BCD16637.)

(archival)

Shelby, North Carolina, 7:30 A.M. eastern: a motel desk clerk knocks on the door. "Is one of y'all's wives expectin'?"

"Yessir!" I yelled.

"She called, said to call her back."

"Thank you, I think she's gonna have that baby!"

Labor not confirmed yet but it's high time. Er, ah, ah, can't wait to wake up, have to set things in motion. I'm a couple of miles from the festival grounds and the nearest possibility of getting a ride to the airport in Charlotte. No use renting a car and driving to Nashville; it's an eight-hour ride. Delta has a flight at 9:20 A.M.

I go next door and wake up Wayne, hoping he had borrowed a car to get back from the festival last night. "Wayne, have you got wheels? Georgia's having a baby."

"Yeah, give me a second to wake up."

I went to make some calls and check out the flights from Charlotte. First I called Georgia, who was sure she was in labor. I had a bunch of notes on different travel scenarios, but flying from Charlotte was pretty straightforward, a Delta flight departing at 9:20. It was coming up on 8:25. The airport was about forty miles away.

Now I'm pacing, drinking coffee and doing arithmetic. Back to Wayne's room, he's conscious and ready to roll. "There's a chance I can make that plane, but we've got to go, go, go," I say. We can't take the car Wayne borrowed to the airport, so it's back out to the festival grounds to see whether Lloyd Johnson, a friend of Wayne's, would be willing to go.

Drive out to the festival park, go to Lloyd's camper to wake him up. "The hell's all this racket?" He's so groggy his crew cut looks messed up.

Wayne says, "Lloyd, Mark's wife's having a baby, we got to see if we can get him to the airport."

Lloyd calls back into the trailer to his wife, "Cath, get some coffee goin', I gotta get the Jeep loose and take this boy to the airport, his wife's havin' a baby!"

Rustling inside the camper. Outside, Lloyd's unhitching the camper from the Jeep. Cathy hands him a cup of coffee, and we're off.

Nowadays, the roads between Shelby and Charlotte are four-lane highways; Google shows it as a forty-five-minute trip. But on July 24, 1982, it was two lanes for the first half of the trip, going through Shelby and Kings Mountain along the way.

Lloyd made it to the Charlotte airport in twenty-eight minutes.

Once we were on the interstate, he poured on the coal, passing people on the left shoulder. I could smell the transmission cooking. I felt the Jeep heel over on two wheels as we rounded a tight curve approaching the terminal at about fifty miles per hour.

We hopped out and ran through the doors. Two ticket agents stood at the desk, shaking their heads. Just missed the 9:20 flight. "Aw, c'mon guys, cut me a break, my wife's having a baby!"

Nope. Just two minutes too late. Lloyd stamped his feet. "Damn! If I'd had my Cadillac you'd 'a made that plane, son, I'd 'a put that sonofabitch in the wind!"

As it turned out, there was a Piedmont flight leaving around noon that arrived in Nashville only a few minutes later than the plane I had missed. I shook hands and thanked the fellas, then settled in to wait for the next plane.

After landing in Nashville, I hustled home to get my car and got to the hospital by 3 P.M. Katherine was born about 5:30 P.M.

I stayed around the hospital until everyone was accounted for and grandparents were notified, then went home to sleep. I returned to the hospital the next morning long enough to hold my new daughter for about thirty minutes before I had to fly back to North Carolina. I got out to the festival park in Shelby for the Sunday afternoon show, handing out cigars.

Monroe's secretary, Betty McInturff, had prepared the band's checks before we left for the trip. Bill handed me my check and said, "That's too much. That's more days than you worked."

Yessir, I said. Bill said, "Don't go spending that. You take that extra day and put it in the bank for that baby."

And I did. (When Katie was eighteen, there weren't very many ways for me to impress her. But she dropped her teen facade when she got eighty dollars from Bill Monroe on her birthday.)

After the show, we hightailed it for Portland, Maine, to take the ferry to Nova Scotia. We had lobster sandwiches for dinner (a choice I would regret later) and boarded the ferry. As we put out to sea, Blake and I smoked my celebratory cigars and watched the lights of Portland fade into the night.

The reality of the last three days had not yet sunk in: the wild ride to the airport, Georgia's labor and the birth of my daughter, and rejoining the band in Shelby for a thousand-mile ride to Maine.

Blake went on to bed, but I stayed up to celebrate and take in the scene on the ship. Once we crossed into international waters, the blackjack and roulette tables were limbered and the lounge grew lively. So did the sea and that lobster sandwich. The end of my night was not a finish to be proud of.

BRIDGEWATER, NOVA SCOTIA, VIA THE EMERGENCY ROOM 55

(recollected)

The morning after a turbulent (for me) passage on the ferry from Portland, Maine, to Nova Scotia, I stood on deck as we coasted into the harbor at Yarmouth. The craggy shoreline was trimmed in mossy spring green in the early sunlight, turning my extraordinary two or three days surreal.

Standing on the pier watching the bus being driven off the ferry, we saw a steel plate on the loading ramp bounce up and knock a hole in the oil pan. "Damn!" Wayne said.

Sure enough, oil was spreading on the ground underneath. So, first thing, we went to a garage to have a patch welded. I was glad to be back in my bunk on a bus that wasn't moving. It was a good episode to nap through.

Then it was off to Bridgewater. Bill had mentioned not feeling well that morning. Now, somewhere along the way, he began moaning. He went to his room for a little while, then came out, looking ashen, and said he thought he needed to go to a hospital.

There's not much between Yarmouth and Bridgewater, but we found the first hospital we could. It was a little place that looked like an empty grade school. It seemed only two or three people worked there. Bill was taken to a room, and we waited while the nurse tried to reach a doctor. Now Bill was shouting in pain.

I had often heard about Monroe's horrific auto accident in 1953, and how, having suffered nineteen broken bones, including his legs and spine, he got out of the ambulance and walked into the emergency room, his legs bowing out because they were so badly shattered. He gave his name at the desk before passing out.

I desperately tried to hurry the nurse. "You don't know this man," I said. "He has a terrific tolerance for pain. He's famous for it. If he is yelling like that, he is about to die!"

He was indeed. His prostate had enlarged and blocked his urethra until his bladder ruptured. He was taken to the hospital in Bridgewater for palliative surgery. WSM sent a jet up to fly him back to Nashville.

But he wouldn't leave before he played in Nova Scotia. Monroe had been booked to play the South Shore Exhibition (like a county fair) in Bridgewater, and the Blue Grass Boys covered the first day and a half without him. But before the concert that night, a van pulled up behind the stage, a wheelchair was unloaded, and a nurse and a doctor put Bill in it and brought him to the stage.

What the hell is he doing here? we all demanded. The nurse said she had told him he could not leave his bed, let alone play a show. But when she returned to his room he was up and dressed. He was very insistent, she said.

That we could believe. We rolled him out to center stage, and he got a huge ovation. He said he had never been to Nova Scotia, and he didn't intend to leave without playing for the folks. Then, groggy with meds, he sang and played "Little Georgia Rose" as if in his sleep.

"Ladies and gentlemen, Bill Monroe!" Wayne called out, and we grabbed the wheelchair and pushed him back to the stage door with emphatic instructions to the medical attendants: "Put his ass in bed!" Wayne barked.

Bill was flown back to Nashville the next day, and the Blue Grass Boys finished the next few days at the fair and covered a couple of more dates in New England. I even sang a couple of tunes.

It was such a strange week for me. I had seen my new daughter for only a few minutes before jetting off and leaving the country. Next, I was in Nova Scotia, more than 1,500 miles away, not knowing whether I'd have a job when I got back.

All of these events had been reported in the Bridgewater press, including that I was a new father. I called home so often the local telephone operators knew me. "It's collect from Mark," I would say, and they would ask, "How's that baby?" At the fair, one of the carnies on the midway spotted me and gave me a huge, pink stuffed poodle, "for the little girl, eh?" When Blake saw it, he went and got another for his little girl. We smuggled them back across the border by stashing them in Bill's stateroom on the bus.

And then . . . after I had returned from Nova Scotia, my parents came to Nashville to see their new grandchild. We went to a Chinese restaurant one night, and as I was pouring a Tsingtao I heard a familiar voice behind me.

"What are you doing drinking that ol' slop?"

I spun around. "Boss, you're supposed to be in the hospital!" I jumped up to shake his hand.

"I had to come in here and get after you," he said.

Recovery can be defined as a return to what you were doing beforehand. Barely three weeks after his ordeal, here Monroe was, catching me with a beer.

A RECORD-BREAKING DISS 56

(archival)

Monroe tipped me about 10 percent for selling his records, and it was a welcome supplement. When I was making sixty dollars per day (on days we had a show), good sales on a two- or three-day trip might amount to an extra day's pay. And during the ten days of Bean Blossom, it really added up.

But then, in 1983, not long before Bean Blossom, I was relieved of those duties, perhaps due to a misunderstanding—or perhaps not.

By that time, I was writing the orders for new stock. Looking to load up before Bean Blossom, I had ordered several units of the live *Bean Blossom* double album. The shipment arrived, but the *Bean Blossom* albums were back-ordered.

When I informed Bill of this, I found he had already looked at the invoice and taken inventory. Where were the *Bean Blossom* albums, he wanted to know. I told him they had been back-ordered, thinking perhaps he missed this detail in the invoice. Well, they charged me for them, he said. Yes sir, I said, and explained that they would ship them when they have them in stock, worrying that I sounded like I thought he was stupid.

Which, in this instance, he might have been. I assured him I did not have them, and I would let him know if I saw them before he did. But he stayed mad about it, and told me to never mind about selling records, he would get someone else to do it.

This was more than just annoying. The ten days of commissions at Bean Blossom was a chunk of change. Fortunately—and surprisingly—Baker, seeing what was happening, jumped right in. Well, by God, you can just sell mine then, he said, and looked at Monroe levelly.

Later, Kenny said it just wasn't right. He said you watch, he'll have Julia selling those records. And that's what happened—Bill put his girlfriend at the record table and paid her.

So that helped a little with my feeling that I had been falsely accused, and the commissions from selling Baker's records took a little of the sting out of it. Also, I didn't have to open as early or close as late as when I was selling Bill's—and sometimes I didn't have to open at all, if it was a small audience.

So, I guess I lost my job to nepotism—probably. On the other hand, when I told my troubles to Monroe's secretary, Betty shook her head. That Bill might not understand the concept of a back order did not surprise her. She told me she had tried to get him to take an agricultural rate on utilities at his farm, a flat rate that would have been far less than what he was paying. But he didn't see the sense in paying for heat in the summertime.

What eventually evolved: now, a certain L. E. White, along with his son and wife, transport and sell Bill's records. Monroe pays their gas and 25 percent of sales. Last night in McAlester, Oklahoma, they sold $700 worth. Gas and incidentals were about $200 and their percentage was $175, so Mon netted $300. He was paying me about 10 percent and transporting the records on his own bus.

Hard to understand.

Pulled into Bean Blossom this time about 4:30 p.m. after a fifteen-hour ride. Straight to the festival park. We haven't had showers in a couple of days. We don't play until noon tomorrow, but we had to come here first. There was no PA for the scheduled start of the show. Meanwhile, L. E. White lagged behind. He was driving James Monroe's old RV, and it broke down four times.

RIVER RANCH RESORT 57

(archival)

In my bunk in the back of the bus at 4:30 A.M., my diesel-infused dreams were interrupted by the driver.

"We're in Montgomery, broke down," Charlie said. "Boss wants you to call them folks and see if they'll fly up here and get us."

The previous plan was Saturday night in Tuscaloosa, Alabama, and Sunday noon near Lake Wales, Florida, at the River Ranch Resort, a rich folks' getaway with its own private airstrip. We were to have met in Ocala, Florida, and be flown in from there.

Now in Montgomery at oh dark thirty, on a bus with a burnt bearing, and with my throat full of cigarette-coffee-diesel phlegm, I can't read the number on the paper, and I'm waking up a guy forty-five minutes after he's gone to bed. Well, I don't feel so hot myself.

We flew out of Montgomery at 7:00 A.M. bound for Tampa, where I was paged as we taxied in. We were met by three people with walkie-talkies, two of whom went after our luggage, the other escorting us to a private apron, where we boarded a twin-prop Beechcraft, blades already turning. Our luggage was already there. We slammed the door, cut in front of a bunch of airliners, and went screaming out of there for the Triple R.

At the ranch airstrip there was a crowd on hand, two state patrol cars with lights flashing, and a Mercedes limo waiting to whisk us to the stage. With a burst of sirens we sped away through the powdery Florida dust.

We arrived backstage twenty minutes before showtime, catching our breath in an air-conditioned trailer, while Hank Williams Jr. wound up his set with a rowdy band that sounded like it had crawled through whiskey and broken glass to get there. (I'll give Hank credit, he had the pipes to get over them.) Then we went out and played an hour-long show that sounded "like slappin' two big boards together," as Monroe put it.

Then we had three-and-a-half hours to kill before a second set, with food and a free bar. Bill ate and rested. Blake ate and observed. Kenny, Wayne, and I drank and drank.

I wound up on a band bus with Willie Nelson's daughter Susie (she said it was an honor to meet me!). I went with another man's wife to go find some Mexican food ("Don't try to do my old lady, OK man?"), and we returned to find him amusedly being accosted by some shameless hussy. I talked big show business with some agent named Joe and told the stage manager if Hank Jr. (who was going to follow us this time) didn't get Bill up onstage early in the set we'll just say fuck it and head for home. (Such language from a Blue Grass Boy!)

By 5:30 P.M. we were getting on a luxurious tour bus that one of the owners had bought one night because he was drunk and wanted it.

Again, we took the VIP route through the airport in Orlando, got on another plane, and chased the Florida sunset back to Tennessee.

On the ground in Nashville, walking through the terminal to baggage claim, Bill had had just about enough of us. Of course, we could tell, so we razzed him a little with some exaggerated weaving and maundering, Wayne slurring, "We in Atlanta yet?"

Now where in hell did I lose my tie?

58 BILL'S BIRTHDAY IN LOUISVILLE

(description of event video)

The Kentucky Fried festival in Louisville was held in September and coincided with Bill's birthday (September 13). It was his seventy-first in 1982, and former Blue Grass Boy Doug Hutchens organized a celebration that featured an onstage presentation of gifts. I had the honor of joining Wayne and Blake to present Bill, on behalf of seventy-two Blue Grass Boys, with a fine, new Stetson hat in a deluxe bandbox.

A procession of alumni Blue Grass Boy fiddlers followed. When Gordon Terry was introduced and strode onstage, Bill chortled and said, "That is really something," his voice choking with emotion. "Gordon Terry, you're breakin' my heart, boy," he said as Terry embraced him. "This is one of the finest Blue Grass Boys that ever worked for me right here, Gordon Terry!" he said. Next came Red Taylor. "There comes another one, friends, there comes one of the great bluegrass fiddlers of all time right there," Bill said of the man who fiddled on the classic recordings of "Rawhide" and "Uncle Pen." "Red, it's so good to see you, man." Red replied, "Bless your heart, I love you to death." "Thank you so much," Bill said, "Be my friend as long as I live, please." Next came Byron Berline. Monroe tugged his suit coat straight and exclaimed, "Powerful!"

Last came Kenny Baker, in the fourteenth year of his tenure with Monroe. Baker, never much for ceremony, wore a half smile and threw a sidelong glance at the crowd as he came on. "Kenny Baker, this is the day, man," Bill said. "Yes it is," Baker replied, shaking Monroe's hand. Bill said, "Thank you for staying with me all down through the years and helping me with the Blue Grass Boys, and being my friend all the way. Don't never let me down, let's stay together as long as we live."

"I never have," Baker said, and ducked out, Blue Grass Boy laughter in the background.

Then Hutchens said, "Bill, we know how much that old mandolin means to you. We've got something here that we think might be a new home for the old mandolin." He stepped forward with a gift-wrapped package.

Terry said, "We got you something, Bill, all the Blue Grass Boys, actually there's quite a few of them, everybody pitched in a little bit of money. Take this case to a higher court."

It was the plush, tooled-leather case emblazoned with his signature that is now enshrined in the Country Music Hall of Fame and Museum.

As Monroe unwrapped it, Terry said, "I was with Bill when he got a little upset with Gibson mandolin," referring to the time Bill gouged out the trademark on the headstock. He had sent it to Gibson for some minor maintenance, and they *refinished* it. So the story goes, Monroe took out a penknife and scraped the new finish off, then carved the Gibson name out of the headstock.

"Look at that," Terry said as Bill held the case. "Ain't that beautiful? That's where that mandolin deserves to be."

Bill looked at the case, then at the crowd, and shook his head, fighting back tears. Baker and Taylor stepped forward to hold it, while Monroe opened it. Terry said, "A mandolin like he's got, 'course he can play any kind and it'd deserve to be in a case like this."

Bill said, "That is wonderful right there, I sure appreciate that boys, you done me a wonderful favor right there. That old mandolin is gettin' old," he said, his voice quivering, and he paused. "But the man that's on it down through the years is gettin' old, Gordon."

"You got another fifty years to go yet," Terry said.

"Please, please pray for me," Bill said.

It had been a rough couple of years—surgeries had laid low a strong, proud man and forced him to confront his mortality. He prayed a lot and made a lot of promises to the Almighty. He gave up a few vices, at least for a time. He still loved to dance, and that was good. But he gave up poker—and that was a damn shame.

59 COUNTRY HARDBALL

(recollected)
One of the few things Bill Monroe and I had in common was baseball. And he loved baseball.

I didn't know him when he had his good fastball. Butch said when he was a kid Bill backed him up against the barn at Bean Blossom and wore him out with the hard stuff.

But Monroe was in his seventies when we first played catch. Still, after a few warm-up tosses, he went through an old-fashioned windup and threw me a curve. I was shocked. "Did you just throw me a curve?" I called. He smiled and threw me another, and it broke the other way. "I can really curve 'em, boy!" he called back.

During the 1940s, when Bill was riding high, his tent shows would roll into towns like the circus, speakers on the roof of a car announcing their arrival. In addition to the music and comedy of the shows, he fielded a baseball team that would take on the local nine.

This was country hardball, and the games were no joke. The Blue Grass Boys team played rawboned coal miners who could hit, pitch, and definitely hurt you. Baker remembered watching baseball as a kid around Jenkins, Kentucky, and the old-timers hollering, "Tar the kilver off'n it!"

Monroe's band was expected to suit up, sometimes with comic results. ("Ask Charlie Cline did he ever get his shoes knocked off at second base!" Monroe would say, still chuckling.) Another time, Paintsville, Kentucky, had a fireballing pitcher, and when Cline's turn to bat came, he was nowhere to be found. Finally, Bill spotted him way up in the last row of seats.

"Charlie, you're up! Come on down here!" Monroe yelled. "Hell no," Charlie yelled back. "I ain't a'battin' against that son of a bitch!"

Freelance writer Jay Feldman was able to finagle a great interview from Monroe about baseball in 1984 ("Bluegrass Baseball"). Often a tough interview, Monroe was standoffish at first. Then he asked Feldman, "Do you expect to make money with this?" Feldman laughed and said, "Well, I certainly hope so!" With that, Bill opened right up. I suppose Feldman had to demonstrate he was no amateur; then Bill accepted him.

Monroe told him band members such as Cline, Clyde Moody, Dave "Stringbean" Akeman, Chubby Wise, Howard Watts (Cedric Rainwater), Don Reno, Jackie Phelps, and G. W. Wilkerson were all pretty good ballplayers. Akeman and Moody were legitimate pro prospects (Moody pitched two seasons with the Dodgers farm club in Asheville, North Carolina), and Phelps was a good shortstop who struck out only three times one season, according to Bill.

For a time Monroe ran two teams: the Blue Grass All-Stars was the traveling squad that would come into town, play a show, then suit up and play the local nine in a night game. Then there was the Blue Grass Ballclub, Monroe's Nashville-based team, which featured a few ringers, semipro and even ex-big-league players. (Bill didn't like to lose.)

That team's greatest game never played was to have been against the (Israelite) House of David, a barnstorming ball club that featured at one time or another such greats as Grover Cleveland Alexander, Mordecai Brown, and Satchel Paige. For reasons unknown, the House of David canceled—which was a shame, because Monroe had lined up country music fan and Hall of Fame pitcher Dizzy Dean as a starter.

"That would have been a great ballgame," Monroe told Feldman. "That House of David, they had a powerful lineup, but Dizzy Dean would have been hard for them to have pulled down."

In the early 1980s, around the same time as Feldman's interview, my Milwaukee Brewers were contenders. In the strike-shortened 1981 season, they were 3–3 against the New York Yankees before losing in a five-game playoff. Bill and I were riding along somewhere on the West Coast and listening to one of the games on the radio as Reggie Jackson came to bat for the Yankees with a man on. First base was open.

"Just walk him," I said.

"They'd better put him on," Monroe said. "That's a powerful man there."

But Milwaukee pitched to him, and sure as hell, Jackson hit a two-run homer.

"What'd I tell you!" Monroe shouted, slapping my shoulder. "How 'bout that, boy!"

"You ain't tellin' me nothin'," I said, chagrined. "I knew they should have walked him."

"Them sorry things had too much of that old slop!" Monroe said.

From then on Bill rooted against the Brewers no matter who they played.

But in 1982, the Brewers and I rallied. Milwaukee looked like it would win its division, needing only to beat the Baltimore Orioles in one of the last four games of the season. Naturally, Bill was rooting for Baltimore. And the Orioles won the first three games.

So, on the last day of the season, it all came down to one game. They were playing in Baltimore at Memorial Stadium; we were playing at Camden Park, an amusement park in Huntington, West Virginia.

It so happened the park had a clown on duty who was a baseball fan. He came backstage to introduce himself and explain that he would be working the crowd as he made his rounds in the park. Monroe didn't pay him much mind, but when he mentioned baseball I chatted him up. I told him I wished there was some way to check on the game. He said his rounds took him past the office every hour or so, and he would look in on the game and relay anything he could.

Monroe said, "They're up against it today, boy! They've got some powerful pitching." Indeed, the Brewers were facing right-hander Jim Palmer (15–5, 3.13 ERA).

After our first set, the clown came by again. "Your shortstop [Robin Yount] hit a home run!" he said. The score was 1–0. Monroe shook his head.

After another set, the clown reappeared. "Your shortstop just hit another home run!" he said. The score was 3–0. I clapped my hands, and Monroe glared at the clown.

Later, between sets, I wandered off into the park and killed some time playing miniature golf. As I was lining up a putt, Blake came trotting up, laughing.

"Your clown came looking for you," he said. Ignorant of Monroe's allegiances, the clown had come backstage to happily deliver the news that the Brewers had won the game 10–2.

That would have annoyed Bill. But the clown wasn't quite through.

Though he hadn't found me, he had run into Blake strolling through the park and told him how he had given Bill the final score. And then, he said, he paid Monroe the greatest compliment he could possibly think of.

"What was that?" Blake asked warily. The clown said, "I told him that while you guys were up there playing, it sounded so good I could just close my eyes and imagine it was Flatt and Scruggs."

"What did he say?" Blake asked, aghast.

The clown said, "I think he was really flattered. He didn't say a thing. He just nodded."

MCCLURE VIA COEBURN 60

(recollected)

In the southwest corner of Virginia, Coeburn (population about two thousand) is the biggest town close to McClure, near where Ralph and Carter Stanley came from and where the Hills of Home Festival is held. When Bill played McClure we would stay in Coeburn, about thirty miles down the hill from the festival grounds at the enticingly named Three-Way Motel.

The name was the best thing about the motel. No doubt it was the swankiest around those parts. Coal country is not long on luxury, and we were in the heart of it. The accommodations were sub-spartan. The bed in my room rested on a frame that was too long, one of the rusty iron mattress rails extending about a foot past the box springs at shin level. After a couple of excruciating whacks, I wrapped a pillow around the rail and cinched it with a belt.

One night I got back to the room after a show, and, before changing out of my suit, I walked over to the gas station next door to buy a soda. I was just taking it from the machine when an old, beat-up car sped into the lot, bouncing over the driveway apron and coming straight at me. It was a Nash Metropolitan, a 1950s subcompact, with a replacement door on the driver's side painted in gray primer. I was about to cut and run when I glimpsed the driver's uniform. Security guard? Police? Deputy?

The unmarked Nash pulled up, and the driver rolled down the window. His passenger was in uniform, too. I was all yes sir, no sir. Just buying a soda, I said, holding out the can. No, sir, I'm from Nashville, working here with Bill Monroe, pointing at the bus. Just got back after a show tonight, up the hill at the Stanley festival. Yes, sir, we're here all weekend. Thanks, y'all have a good evening.

Alright. They sped off.

When I got back to the room, I told Baker what had just happened. Having grown up just over the mountain in Jenkins, Kentucky, he provided local insight. "Ah, it's that damned suit," he said. "They've been having some labor trouble up at the mines here lately. They probably thought you were some out-of-town lawyer or union guy. I'll be damned."

Baker was pro-union. He'd been a coal miner. He'd say, "Now, by God, a lot of these people bad-mouthing the union don't remember what it was like before. That Tennessee Ernie Ford song '16 Tons'? That's how it was, son, you bought your food and clothes and paid your rent at the company store. They keep on tearin' down the union and that's how it'll be again."

When people say, "way back in the hills," they mean places like this. If you surveyed the festivalgoers and saw someone who looked fairly "normal," they probably were not from around here. Whether the result of coal mining, poverty, a shrinking gene pool, bad water, or bad luck, locals were afflicted by various deformities—odd facial proportions, strange jawlines, or just the look of having been "kicked by a mule," as Blake put it.

Playing Ralph's festival was usually a long three- or four-day stand. Most bluegrass festivals are rustic, but the McClure fester was especially rugged, with rough-hewn planks for audience seating and troughs for latrines.

The stage was at the bottom of a steep-sided hollow that formed a cone-shaped amphitheater. Even for a young man, descending to the stage while carrying a bass was tricky. Every longtime festivalgoer had to tell me about the time after a rain when Ralph's bass player, Jack Cooke, slipped in the mud at the top and slid all the way to the bottom on his back, holding his bass in the air.

The place is known as Smith Ridge, and there's not a level spot on it. Now, Ralph and Carter Stanley are both buried not far from the stage. (I'll never think of that place without remembering the well-known story of Melvin Goins talking to Ralph, looking up at the graveyard, and saying, "Poor old Carter. Reckon he's rottenin' by now?")

After Carter died, Larry Sparks was the first to succeed him on guitar and lead vocal. Later, Sparks formed his own band. McClure was his home crowd, and he seemed more confident there, forceful and charismatic. I saw him one night when the evening mist coalesced into ground fog down at the edge of the stage, wafting around the footlights and making everything look spooky. Sparks's set was like a seance. With his black suit, hair slicked back from a widow's peak, and mournful singing as sepulchral as any Stanley anthem, he had the home folks howling.

For an anonymous sideman from Wisconsin, conversations up on that mountain were hard to find. I had begun to get the hang of various southern accents, but the dialect in this remote area, with its archaic constructions, antique vocabulary, and clipped cadence, was hard to make out. It seemed a vestige of the Scots-Irish (Irish, actually) who washed up into the Appalachian hills and never came down.

I knew a little of this from my dad, who grew up in Western North Carolina, an isolated area before the interstate was blasted through the Smoky Mountains. He didn't speak with an accent anymore, but he understood it. He couldn't offer me much advice, except to tell me to listen closely and pay attention to what was *not* being said.

Putting together what I experienced and what I knew about Dad, I'd say the archetypal mountaineer can be a "caution": suspicious of strangers, quick to take offense, and difficult to reason with. If they like you they'll do anything for you. On the other hand, if they don't like you they probably never will. If you've offended them, they will never forget it. And if you offend them badly enough, they will flat kill your ass.

61 ROLL ON BUDDY

(archival)

It's a long way to Harlan. It's a long way to Hazard. Just to get a little brew . . .

In Eastern Kentucky, in coal country, there are dry counties where men get double drunk, and places where the rule of law goes only as far as the nearest sheriff's deputy.

In Jackson, Kentucky, Bill warned me about going into town. "The law 'round here is awful bad," he said. He told me when they tried to put on a bluegrass festival here, county and city police harassed the performers. If someone came in after a long drive and was parked backstage, sleeping in their car, they'd be arrested for vagrancy. "Drug 'em right out of the car," Bill said.

So don't spit on the sidewalk in Jackson. And for God's sake, don't get crossways with any of the good old boys. In 1974, Ralph Stanley's lead singer Roy Lee Centers (who channeled Carter's voice so amazingly) was taken out in the country and murdered in front of his own son. I asked Junior Blankenship, Ralph's lead guitar player, what the hell happened. "Buncha ol' boys took him out one night and kilt him, I reckon," was Junior's incurious reply.

"Didn't anything ever come of it? Didn't anybody do anything about it?" I asked.

"You mean the law? That *was* the law," Junior said.

It's actually a much longer story, but Junior told the gist of it. The killer was a local land developer and a sheriff's deputy. His personal attorney was the prosecutor. The murderer spent little more than a month in jail.

Don't spit on the sidewalk there.

Tonight we played at the Breathitt County Coliseum, a semicircular, blue-and-gray concrete basketball arena. Bill Monroe and Ralph Stanley topped the marquee. The audience was a hard lot, mostly miners and their families. There wasn't a lot of foolishness about them. Small talk and little jokes at the record table drew a steady, unsmiling stare.

These folks were here for little else but the music, which wasn't easy to hear in this hard-walled echo chamber. The Wilson Brothers led off the show, strictly adhering to the Stanley style. Of special note was "The Stanleys Will Sing Again," a tribute to Ralph's late brother, Carter, sung to the tune of "Mother's Not Dead (She's Only Sleeping)."

No alcohol was sold on the premises, but it wasn't needed. There was plenty in the parking lot. A drunk collared me. "What's your daddy's name?"

"Gilbert," I said. "Gilbert Hembree."

No reaction—an unsatisfactory answer. "You ain't the one I want to talk to." He shuffled off. I figured it was probably for the best.

Stanley and his band are the local favorites, and they wow the crowd. It's a wild, yelling mess, and the crowd loves it, dancing on sheets of plywood laid down to protect the hardwood floor A local clogging team, the Black Diamonds, takes the floor. With their uniforms and fierce demeanor, the youngsters remind me of a drum and bugle corps.

After the Stanley set, a local DJ steps up to the mike and, with ear-splitting enthusiasm, screams, "Now here's Santy Claus to make the presentation of the governor's citation to Bill Monroe, Ralph Stanley, and the Wilson Brothers!"

A guy in a Santa suit steps up to hand off framed certificates. Next comes the raffle. Two solemn fellows receive a coffeemaker and a chainsaw.

Next comes Bill Monroe, the headliner. We're on the floor in the middle of this arena, playing to about 25 percent of the circle, and the sound caroms crazily. Circular concrete arenas are like that; once the sound travels past the center and hits the opposite wall, it splinters into tangents, secants, and chords. The echoes return to the stage at different times in an unintelligible jumble. I can hear the bass echo from the front, and a moment later from behind. You can ignore these extraneous sounds if you have monitors or can hear the guy next to you. I have neither.

Kenny and Wayne have put in plenty of parking-lot time before the show and are thus anesthetized. Wayne flashes his big smile and flails his guitar. Kenny, red-faced and sardonic, jigs away from his mike in disgust and walks off to talk to some women standing at the rail on the edge of the court.

In front of us, folks are dancing up a storm, all knees and elbows, buck 'n' wing, clogging, flopping, and flying, some of them falling down in their frenzy. Overwhelmed in the sonic maelstrom, adrift and bobbing in a tempest of slapback and echoes, I become aurally disoriented—I have no idea of where I am in relation to the band, or they to me.

Like a man overboard, I call out "Help!" Over at the Stanley record tables, Jack Cooke doubles over laughing. (From then on, anytime he saw me he would holler, "Hayyyylp!") Monroe gives me a solo, jumping and screaming and fanning my bass with his hat. Someone asks for "Roll in My Sweet Baby's Arms," and I sing tenor while Bill dances with a little girl.

For the grand finale, all three bands play. There is no chance of music. Kenny is sawing away like Doug Kershaw, weaving badly, and everyone is screaming.

After the show we find the brakes on the bus are frozen. Even for the mountains in December, fifteen degrees is unusually cold. The driver piles newspaper up against the wheels and sets it afire, smoke and sparks rising to the night sky and a full moon. (Aha! A full moon. That explains tonight.)

While this is going on, Ralph's lead singer Charlie Sizemore and I confer and commiserate on tonight's ordeal. "Seniority leads to insanity, I reckon," he says, spitting chaw into a Dixie cup. "I didn't really plan to get into music. You could say I just kind of lucked into it."

PART VIII
"OVER THE WAVES"

(partly archival)

In 1983, we toured Europe with a country music package show promoted by Mervyn Conn and featuring, among others, Skeeter Davis, Roy Drusky, Jim & Jesse, Jeannie Pruett, Porter Wagoner, Billy Walker, Narvel Felts, Tammy Wynette, Jerry Lee Lewis, Boxcar Willie, Don Williams, Faron Young, and the Dillards.

The first stop was in London at the International Festival of Country Music, held in Wembley Arena. The foreign nature of country music abroad was on full display as the fandom at Wembley indulged in a sort of cowboy cosplay I had never seen, with British fellows walking around in chaps and western hats, and carrying six-shooters. In the spirit of things, Peter Rowan (ex–Blue Grass Boy), who happened to be touring England at the same time, appeared backstage dressed as a gaucho wearing a big sombrero, a poncho, pink tights, and boots. Bill caught sight of him, turned on his heel, and pointedly ignored him.

Peter came to me. "Hey, I've got a driver and I know a great Indian restaurant with a nice pub right next door. Wanna go, Blue Grass Boy?"

Oh yeah, you bet! We had a terrific meal and a lot of fun trading Blue Grass Boy stories.

From there it was on to Cork, in southern Ireland. Incredibly, this was Bill's first trip to the land from which so much fiddle music has come. Although there were many on the show who were considered bigger stars in the United States, this was Bill's night.

When he was introduced, the audience went through the roof! Bill stood tall at center stage, taking it all in, then threw his head back and bellowed, "Halloooooooo, Ireland!" The crowd roared. "I have waited so long to be here! And the Blue Grass Boys are ready to go!"

Kenny tore into the intro, and the audience went wild. It was bedlam. People were streaming down the aisles to take pictures. They shrieked like schoolgirls during instrumental breaks. They laughed out loud watching our choreography around a single vocal mike. They roared again when Bill introduced Baker, "the Greatest Fiddle Player in Bluegrass Music," and they shook the building in time to "Jerusalem Ridge." I thought this must be what it was like for the Beatles.

It was quite a show, but the celebration was only starting. Afterward, at the Metropole Hotel, there would be three floors full of revelry.

We got back and changed clothes, and Baker and I headed downstairs for a drink. As we approached, a cheering throng poured out of the lounge into the lobby, engulfed Baker, and swept him away like a riptide. I wouldn't see him again for a couple of days. They took him out to some castle in the country, where he was wined and dined as he held court and people bore him gifts.

I continued to the bar and was immediately taken up by a couple of local characters who bought me a Beamish ale and showed me an Irish bar trick they like to play on foreigners: Beamish, brewed locally and served as a live ale there in the city, has such a thick head that you can lay a coin on it and it won't sink. To demonstrate, they asked me to give them a coin. When I pulled a dime out of my pocket they said, no, that's too easy.

That they may have attached themselves to me as a ticket into the party mattered not to me. I was glad for the company, and I enjoyed the local flavor (including the Beamish).

What an uproar at the Metropole that night! People were climbing the drainpipes to get in, I heard. It was definitely the place to be in Cork. I saw well-heeled gentlemen in three-piece suits rolling about on the floor singing drinking ditties.

As a Blue Grass Boy, I was granted full access to all the bars and lounges on all the floors, and people bought me a Beamish wherever I went. And it went down easy. Not as bitter as Guinness, it was like drinking Malt-O-Meal (chocolate porridge is how I translated that for my Irish drinking buddies). And there is no hangover the next morning, save for a horrible taste from all that happy live ale having died in your mouth during the night. ("Ah, yes, the Beamish breath!" my Irish friends said the next day.)

At one point in the evening, a handsome young man in a tuxedo intro-duced himself as my personal bodyguard. I saw no need. Oh no, he said, on a night like this the place will be full of thieves and rogues. I eyed him— slight build, no bigger than I. You don't look much like a bodyguard, I said. "Karate. Green belt," he assured me.

I learned later this was a middling rank of karate. Nevertheless, I allowed him to accompany us, and I had to admit he was quite helpful, striding up to the bar authoritatively, holding up his hand to order while invoking a sponsor's name, calling out, "Three here! Carling!" and returning with a platter of beer.

Ergo, we drank for free, and freely. One of my Irish companions, Colm Murphy, an artist of some repute and a well-known man about town, allowed that though I drank rather more slowly, I put on a good show for a Yank, at Beamish yet.

As the evening went on, I learned that in Ireland there is no such thing as closing time when you're with the right people. (Same in England, I hear.) The rooms become more exclusive, but if you have standing you will be invited, as I was. About four in the morning, I learned the fellow in the tux was neither bodyguard nor security person, and in fact had no affiliation with the hotel or any of the sponsors. He was a professional actor. (He did own the tux.)

It seems our exploits made the news in local music circles. On the following Sunday afternoon, Blake (who does not drink) and I were invited to Sir Henry's Pub for an open-mike folk music jam session, and hence earned even more fame. Though Blake was playing an open-back banjo that had been handed to him, and I couldn't play much guitar, they went crazy right from the time I leaned into a mike and said, "Howdy!" The way off the stage was blocked by pints of Beamish. (My reputation!) We passed them out to the audience, further endearing ourselves.

Wherever we went, people would stop us to laugh and slap us on the back. Walking out to a small plane the next morning, we were even recognized by the baggage crew on the tarmac.

On our last night in Cork, a gentleman handed me a mason jar of poitín— Irish moonshine, made from potatoes. I swirled the jar, as my father had taught me, to see the ring of bubbles at the top that indicates it's genuine and properly fermented, and (hopefully) won't make you go blind. Thanking the man, I told him I could not accept it. We would be flying to Belfast the next day, and I expected security would take our baggage apart. In fact, the itinerary we received from the tour managers specifically mentioned Belfast and cautioned against carrying contraband. And I guessed poitín is no more legal in Northern Ireland than moonshine is in the States.

Don't worry, the Irishman said. Make sure it's at the top of your bag. Don't try to hide it. That just annoys them. If they ask, tell them it's a gift.

So, I decided to give it a try. When we deplaned at Belfast, baggage inspection was held at the end of the Jetway, before we even entered the terminal. When my turn came, I put my bag on the table and opened it for the guard. He pulled out the mason jar.

"What's this, then?" he demanded.

"It's a gift," I replied.

He held the jar up and swirled it, and a bead of bubbles formed at the top. He grinned and said, "Very good, sir!" and put the jar back in the bag.

I brought that 'shine all the way back to the States, and it stayed in my cupboard for years. It was awful.

63 BILL GETS HIS ENCORE

(archival)

Ireland was the high point of our European tour with Mervyn Conn's country music extravaganza. After that came dates in Germany, in Essen and Frankfurt, and a final date in Zürich.

The other stars of the show now held greater sway, although we got a great reception in Frankfurt. There were a lot of US servicemen on hand, and Bill had a good spot, later in the show. By the end of our set, the crowd was clapping and stomping. Bill paused at the edge of the stage, expertly timing the right moment to walk back out for his encore.

Just as Bill started forward, the Irish fellow who was stage manager held out his hand to stop him—a brave move if he had known how dangerous it is to step between Bill and the stage if that's where he's headed. "There's no time," he said. "We have to bring Tammy on."

And so Bill yielded to Tammy Wynette.

The next night, we were at an arena in Zürich, getting ready to play a set just before intermission, when the same stage manager appeared in the dressing room. "Right, then, there's been a slight change in the schedule. You'll be going on first after the intermission."

I don't know what made me think I could get away with it, but I tore into the guy. "Look, you screwed Bill out of an encore last night, and now you're gonna send ten thousand people out for a hot dog and bring us on? Who the hell's idea was this?"

"Mervyn Conn!"

"Oh, bullshit! Nobody's seen him around anywhere. But if he's here, you go tell Mr. Conn that Bill Monroe, the Father of Blue Grass Music and a member of the Country Music Hall of Fame, wants to go on before the intermission!"

The guy went back out. The room was silent. While I was ripping this guy, Monroe had turned his back and played his mandolin into a corner. Now Baker chuckled and said, "By God, Mark's my horse if he don't never win a race."

In a few minutes the stage manager returned.

"I've spoken to Mervyn," he said.

"Oh, bullshit!"

"He says you may go on before the intermission."

"Oh. Ok." I smiled. "Thank you."

When we arrived at the stage, I stopped smiling. We were to follow Rose Marie, a European act that was more rock than country. Later, an audio crewman told me the sound had been measured at 110 decibels at the back wall—only a little less noisy than an airliner taking off. What have I done, I thought. We're going to get up there with no amps, nothing plugged in, just mikes, and we're going to sound like peashooters.

But I had not accounted for Bill. The stage manager's slight had not been forgotten, and Big Mon was ready to prove a point.

When we got onstage, he swelled up to twice his size—the Incredible Bill. Every move was huge. You couldn't stand within ten feet of him. During a banjo break, he was hammering his mandolin in Blake's ear and screaming, "Burn 'em up! Tear 'em up!" strutting about, doing the Pete Townshend windmill move, leaping from one end of the stage to the other, absolutely *killing* that audience.

At the end of the set, the cheering crowd held lighters aloft and chanted for more. I looked to the stage manager, eyebrows raised. He rolled his eyes and waved us on for an encore.

Back at the hotel after the show, Bill sat at a table in the lobby and signed autographs for more than an hour. I waited in line, still in my suit, hat in hand. Others offered to let me go ahead, but I shook my head and told them I was just a fan.

When I finally got to Bill, he looked up, surprised. I shook his hand and said, "Boss, I put you in one hell of a spot today, and I'm sorry about that. But I'll be damned if you didn't come through like a champ. I've never seen the beat of it. I've never seen anyone that could do what you did today."

He smiled slightly and said, "Not many men can."

64   A WONDERFUL SCHOOL OF MUSIC

(recollected)

Touring Europe with a package show gave us time to converse with other country musicians that we normally would not see much. Aside from the leaders, we were all sidemen. But some of the guys working with bigger stars—Tammy Wynette, for instance—looked down on us.

One fellow got his just deserts from Blake. Now, Blake is about as pleasant a person as you will ever meet. But when this guy got a little snooty, Blake asked mildly, "Do y'all record with her, then?"

Well, er, ah, no. On recordings, such luminaries were always backed by A-Team session players, the big guns like Buddy Emmons on steel and Pig Robbins on piano. Those guys didn't have to leave town to make their money. Sidemen were hired for road work.

It was different for the Blue Grass Boys. Bill's band traveled with him, did most TV appearances with him, and recorded his albums with him.

"Bluegrass is a wonderful school of music," Monroe often said. Some may think that was just a cheery way for Bill to promote his patriarchal role in the genre. But, actually, it's true. You can't just play canned stuff, read a score, or concentrate on your own part to play bluegrass. You must master the fundamentals: time, rhythm, pitch, harmony, and dynamics, along with improvisational skills and a thorough knowledge of the music's style and lineage, the traditional fiddle tunes and the old songs.

Good bluegrass musicians, more than in other genres, are stand-alone performers. They don't need a drummer. They don't need a click track. They don't need a score, chord charts, or written arrangements. Each of them can stand on their own two feet and carry a tune, improvise a solo, or play along and match other players step for step. They know how to complement a soloist or a lead singer.

Once you know how to play bluegrass, you can hold your own. You can excel in other styles.

It's a wonderful school of music.

THE BLUE GRASS GOYS IN ISRAEL 65

(recollected)

For a few thousand dollars, would you go on a ten-day vacation in Israel with Bill Monroe, Mac Wiseman, Boxcar Willie, Wendy Holcombe, and evangelist preacher Jimmie Snow?

That's OK, no one else would either—except for the half-dozen people who actually signed on for the trip. Given the poor advance sales, Mac and Boxcar bowed out early. But plans proceeded. The perk for the Blue Grass Boys was that spouses would be allowed to come along, expenses paid. Blake and Wayne brought their wives. I made a pitch to Georgia, but our daughter was about a year old so that was out of the question.

It was touted as the first bluegrass music tour in Israel. In the weeks leading up to departure, Monroe would tell audiences, "We're gonna go to the Holy Land, and we're gonna sing the gospel. And I just hope they accept it."

I wanted to tug his elbow and tell him, "Uh, Bill, there's gonna be a lot of Jewish people there."

Still, it was a terrific trip I could never afford otherwise, with both profound and hilarious moments. Lest you think me an inveterate wise ass, I will say there were several times I was moved by Bill's spirituality, and a few times that I shared these moments of deep reflection.

To many people, an ancient historical site is no more than a pile of rocks. But at places like Masada and Tel Megiddo, after the others had headed back to the bus or on to the next thing, Bill and I lingered, soaking up the vibes, the residual energies that permeate such places.

At the Western Wall in Jerusalem, visitors were required to cover their heads; paper kippahs were handed out to tourists who needed them. Bill's western hat sufficed. I watched from afar as he stood at the wall and laid his hands on the massive stones. He stayed there awhile, towering above the devout who surrounded him, conspicuous in his blue suit and white straw hat.

What many fans heard about this trip was that Bill Monroe was baptized in the Jordan River. This was a pivotal event in his faith after his near-death experiences. He had sworn to repent, and the baptism meant so much to him—absolution in the Jordan River of song and scripture—that it was hard to stand by and not be moved. I know he cherished the moment.

Bill was accompanied to the Holy Land by Dee Dee Prestige, later Diana Christian, née Delores Bacon, a singer from Brainerd, Minnesota, who moved to Duluth, and thence to Nashville, to take her turn trying to catch the brass ring in the music business.

She was dressed for the part—knee-high white patent leather boots, fringed skirt and western-style blouse, and a cowgirl hat perched on a mountain of wavy, raven hair.

This attire wouldn't have drawn untoward attention at the Opry or any country music venue. But as we walked through the labyrinthine streets of Jerusalem's Muslim Quarter, it was shocking. Women in hijabs gasped, threw their hands over their mouths, and scurried indoors. Men made cat noises. Monroe locked arms with Dee Dee and marched along, and the look on his face suggested that the first person to say something in English was going to get punched in the nose.

How the Israelis felt about our music was hard to tell. At a concert in Tiberias, they seemed distracted, talking among themselves, although they did clap along when we played "Jerusalem Ridge." Something about a minor key, I guess.

Bill didn't really understand them either. I won't claim to be smart enough not to fire up a cigarette at the dinner table on a Friday night. ("Shabbat," the waiter said softly, handing me an ashtray as he asked me to refrain from smoking.) But Bill could not understand why he couldn't have a glass of milk with his steak. And having to choose between an entrée and the dairy buffet in the hotel restaurant really had him flummoxed.

But we had some fun, too. When we came down from Masada, everyone, except for Bill and Kenny, went swimming in the Dead Sea.

When we visited the Church of the Nativity in Bethlehem, Pastor Snow's wife was appalled at its Byzantine splendor. All the icons and ornate carvings dripping with gold were so much idolatry and graven imagery to her.

I explained that these things were crafted by the finest artists and tradesmen of the day, the greatest sculptors, painters, metalsmiths, and so on, who would have considered their works the highest form of worship they could summon. Here, in the Church of Nativity, you might think of these things as gifts to the baby Jesus, just as the Three Wise Men brought gold, frankincense, and myrrh.

"Oh, I'm so sorry," she said. "Are you Catholic?" No, I said, refraining from telling her no, not anymore. Quit while you're ahead, I say.

That's more than the Blue Grass Boys could do on this trip. I'm sure the airfare and five-star hotels made this an exorbitantly expensive trip. But it was a busman's holiday. We were never paid for any of the shows.

At the baggage claim back in Nashville, Bill came around and shook hands with all the band. "Boys, you never done a man no bigger favor than this," he said.

"That's for goddam sure," muttered Baker.

PART IX
"LIVE AND LET LIVE"

(recollected)

We were about to play an outdoor concert in downtown Pittsburgh when a terrific thunderstorm blew through and knocked out the power. Downtown went dark, and it rained cats and dogs.

Even after the storm, it looked like a rainout. No sound company wants to deploy its gear when everything's wet, and musicians are not crazy about walking around on an electrified stage with wet feet.

Still, we hadn't left the stage area, and a number of fans were scattered throughout the seating area awaiting a formal postponement.

Of course, the Blue Grass Boys don't have to plug in to play. So, Bill went onstage and shouted to the remaining people that he was proud to be in Pittsburgh and he meant to play for the folks. "Come on up here and gang around, and the Blue Grass Boys will play for you here tonight," he called out.

Perhaps fifty or sixty people, slowly at first and then eagerly, stepped up on the big stage and seated themselves in a semicircle around the band. When we launched into the first tune, they exchanged delighted looks, incredulous at their good fortune. *Au naturel* really is the best way to hear a bluegrass band, for the band as well as the audience. We had a great time, and the people loved it.

The evening air was hot and humid, so when we boarded the bus after the show we opened the windows to get some circulation going as we began to roll out of town. All the band was sitting up front, still dressed, and the banter was lively and pleasant, with Bill feeling good about the show.

We were at a stoplight when, through the open windows, we heard a guy in the car next to us yell, "What the hell kind of band is this without Sammy Bush!"

We looked at each other. Who in hell says that to the Blue Grass Boys?

"Let's get him!" Wayne said. The driver said, "You boys need the door?" Yeah, we said, lining up in the aisle and cocking our hats. "You gonna go our bail?" Wayne called over his shoulder to Monroe. "Yessir!" he said, bringing up the rear as we filed forward.

The door swung open, and here came the Blue Grass Boys in full regalia, suits, ties, hats, and all, with Bill right behind.

The guy in the car looked up, eyes wide and jaw dropped. Then he peeled out, blowing the red light.

We got back on the bus, still laughing. That was one of the few times I ever heard Bill really guffaw.

67 FEATS OF MAGIC

(recollected)

Several in the first generation of bluegrass music have become legends known simply by their first names: Lester and Earl; Ralph and Carter; Jim and Jesse; Bobby and Sonny; Mac; and of course, Bill. When Bill Keith played banjo in his band, Monroe called him Brad. Because there is only one Bill.

Such greats do not earn an undisputed title or steadfast worship without a little hocus-pocus. Saints are required to have performed at least one miracle. Even Jesus Christ pulled a few tricks out of his garment to help make his case.

Though I never saw or heard of Bill performing any resurrections, I did see a few things I still can't believe. If you are a Monroe fan, you may have heard a few of these tales. And, like me, you may be surprised to find out how many of them are actually true.

But miracles need little introduction. Here's a list:

Commanding the heavens: At Bean Blossom and many other festivals, Bill sometimes seemed to control the weather. When it came time for his set, the rain would stop. If it was night, the moon would rise. If it was overcast, the sun would come out—and when it did, a shaft of sunlight would fall through the trees and hit him like a spotlight. Any of these things might strike you as coincidental until you saw them happen again and again.

Shape-shifting: This was something that became even more apparent when Bill was feeling poorly. Once he was offstage, you could see his stature sag as he returned to normal dimensions. But onstage, especially in front of a big crowd, he became larger than life. All of his movement and motions were scaled to the size of the venue. In a big place, you couldn't be near him onstage. You had to stand back.

Walking on water: I had heard more than once about how Bill could wear a white suit while walking through a muddy field at a festival and arrive at the stage without a speck on his shoes. In fact, at a waterlogged quagmire in Canada, I tried to follow exactly in his footsteps. I had a pair of cheap, shiny plastic shoes (the kind you get with a tuxedo rental) for just such conditions. By the time I got to the stage, they needed to be hosed off. But Bill pulled a small swatch of newspaper out of his coat pocket, leaned on a wall with his other hand, and reached down to give one toe a little swipe.

I asked Baker, whose shoes were in about the same shape as mine, how the hell Bill could do that. He shook his head and said he didn't know, but he'd seen him do it many times.

And then there was Bill's uncanny—nay, supernatural—timing.

For example, Sam Bush, hero of newgrass, represented a new generation in contrast to Bill and all things traditional. Sam's bands had long hair and beards, they didn't wear uniforms, and their instruments were wired up, plugged in, and amplified.

Monroe might have been less exasperated by Sam if he didn't recognize his immense talent. It just bugged Bill that someone who could play like Sam would play the way he did. "He knows that ain't right," Bill would say.

But when Sam was in the hospital for cancer surgery, Bill called him to wish him well and offer any help he could. And when a benefit was held for Sam at a club on the west side of town, Wind in the Willows, Bill asked us to go with him to play the show after our last Opry spot.

As soon as we finished our Opry set and got back to the dressing room, we packed up our instruments and headed across town in two or three cars. We all arrived at about the same time, but Bill was a few yards ahead of us as we walked across the lawn to the entrance. We saw the doorway light up and heard the audience roar.

Inside the club, the concert was just ending. A couple of encores had been played, and John Hartford was thanking everyone for coming when suddenly the spotlight swung around—and there was Bill Monroe, transfigured in the doorway. The place went crazy.

The moment was perfect, and I know Bill could not have timed it on purpose. I was with him, and if it hadn't been for hauling a bass I might have walked through the door before him. We all simply got there as soon as we could. But Bill arrived at *exactly* the right moment, as if on cue, to the greatest possible dramatic effect.

A few days later, friends visiting Sam in the hospital were showing him a video of the concert. He was joking that he had always said he'd give his left nut if he could sing like Bill, and now that he had he still couldn't sing tenor. But toward the end of the video, he was begging off, telling his friends he needed to get some rest. Just wait a minute, they said, you've got to see this.

And then came Bill's appearance. Sam buried his head in a pillow, beating the bed with his fist and screaming, "I can't laugh! I can't laugh!"

68 PTL: *PASS THE LOOT*

(recollected)

Once upon a time in South Carolina, just across the North Carolina state line from Charlotte, there was a fundamentalist Christian theme park called Heritage USA.

It was the high-water mark for televangelists Jim and Tammy Faye Bakker, who parlayed their TV ministry into a worldwide satellite network collecting more than $1 million per week from devout viewers. In its day—from 1978 to its bitter end in 1989—it was ranked as the third-most attended theme park in the world, trailing only the Disney parks in Florida and California.

The 2,300-acre park comprised a five-hundred-room hotel, four-hundred-site campground, amphitheater, Bible school, timeshare condos, skating rink, water park, church, and Main Street USA, a nostalgic avenue resembling a movie set. Strung overhead were affirmative banners such as "Victory Today!" (Even Blake, a religious man himself, asked, "Who are we fighting?")

And, of course, there was the television production studio, which was where we taped an appearance on the *PTL Club*, a Christian talk show grown out of the *700 Club* (and later reclaimed by Jerry Falwell after Jim Bakker had his fall from grace—or, I should say, after his fall from grace became public).

The show was taped live in front of a studio audience. After we had finished our first segment we remained onstage, off camera, as the program continued. Jim and Tammy Faye were not present (out shopping, perhaps). In their stead, a second-string preacher came out, greeted the audience, and began to testify. Still standing, we settled in for the sermon.

Next to me was Kenny Baker. Like my dad and many others his age who had moved out of the Appalachians, he'd had his fill of fire and brimstone at an early age. I recall a Sunday morning at a festival in Chatom, Alabama, 9 A.M., already so hot the bus windows were fogging up. Baker and I had just stepped out to get some coffee when the preacher onstage checked the mike, then kicked off the services at top volume. "Praise God!" he bellowed. Baker ran me over to get back on the bus, muttering, "It's too goddam early for this shit!"

So, we braced ourselves for the PTL benediction. As the preacher spoke, a collection was being taken up. Large popcorn buckets were passed along each row, and people were dropping big money in them—not fives or tens. More like fifties and hundreds.

The preacher was heating up. "We know that *sahntists* say the *left* sahd o' yo' brain controls the *raht* side o' yo' body. *Sahntists*. Say. That's what they say. An' *sahntists* say that the *raht* sahd o' yo' brain controls the *left* sahd o' yo' body. *Sahntists*. Say."

A dramatic pause.

I leaned over and whispered in Baker's ear, "And your asshole controls this entire outfit."

Baker wheeled and disappeared into the wings. "Where'd he go?" Bill whispered. "I think he got choked," I murmured, holding my hand to my throat.

After the sermon, I found Baker out on the loading dock, smoking a Lucky. Chuckling and dabbing at his eyes, he said, "Goddammit, son, don't you *ever* do that to me again! You're gonna get us *both* fired!"

69 BLUEGRASS AND THE HIPPIES

(partly archival)

Bill didn't care much for all the long hair and beards and bare feet, but he definitely would accept tickets from hippies who wanted to attend Bean Blossom. In fact, attendance at his festival was greatly bolstered by young folks from nearby Bloomington, home of Indiana University.

But it took him awhile to catch up. In the 1960s, he had hipsters in the band. But nobody knew what that smell from the back of the bus was then, at least not at first. Richard Greene kept a pack of Indian cigarettes around to serve as an explanation. "We were just stupid kids," Peter Rowan recalled, ignorant of the fact that the slipstream around a moving bus carries air from the rear to the front, out through the vent windows at the driver's seat, or to any other open windows up front.

It was only a matter of time. From the first bluegrass festival, at Fincastle, Virginia, in 1965, younger folks were a mainstay of the audience. The old-timers were there, but it was the younger crowd that boosted attendance into the thousands and then tens of thousands. Some of the smoke rising from such gatherings was not from Indian cigarettes.

To be sure, smoking dope was not legal or widely tolerated at most bluegrass festivals. But it happened, and when first-generation pickers' kids got old enough it became a fact of life—not approved of, but not all that unusual.

With the next generation came different takes on the music. Again, it was only a matter of time. But the first generation was not amused, and there was friction. They didn't like the long hair and beards, and the new stylings were an aberration. "That ain't no kind of music," as Bill said. The old-timers and good ol' folks in the audience didn't care much for the new crowd, either. If some band ventured too far afield, Blake would observe, "That oughtta set them lawn chairs to snappin'."

But the new generation kept coming into its own, and the benefits of soaring attendance and growing record sales were undeniable. Despite whatever personal opinions Bill held, he had to admit the hip crowd's money spent as well as anyone's.

He still scoffed at outlandish, riff-driven playing. He would rail about disrespect for the old fiddle tunes, with hot players like Sam Bush and Vassar Clements turning the traditional melodies inside out. Vassar, an ex–Blue Grass Boy, would be mentioned by name in these rants. "*Why* would he put them notes in there?" Bill would say. "That's a bunch of stuff, boy. And that Vassar, now he's a powerful fiddler. He knows 'Sally Goodin' don't go that way, and *why* would he put them crazy notes in there?"

Once, when Vassar came offstage, Bill asked him what number he was just playing. "Turkey in the Straw," Vassar replied. Monroe said, "Sht! There wasn't no turkey inside a hundred miles of that!"

And then there was my own time with Baker. We had played *Austin City Limits*, and Peter Rowan was backstage. As we got ready to leave, Peter shook my hand and put about half a joint in my palm. "Careful," he said. "Try one and wait a bit to see where you're at."

When I got back to my hotel room, I took his advice. And he was right. I snuffed out the remainder, slipped it into a pack of cigarettes, and went down the hall to Baker and Wayne's room, where the party was. In the midst of the party, I ran out of cigarettes and stupidly discarded the (not quite) empty pack.

The next morning, I realized what I had done. I even thought I remembered setting the empty pack on a dresser among the empty cans and ashtrays. I went to breakfast and mulled my fate. Maybe it got thrown away without a second glance. If the room hadn't been cleaned, maybe it was still there.

On the way back from breakfast I ran into Bill Holden, banjo player and former Blue Grass Boy, who had come around to visit. They found it, he said. What did they do with it, I wondered. Holden shrugged and wished me luck.

Well, there it was. And I figured it could be a firing offense. There was nothing else to do but go face the music.

When I got to their room, Baker was up and Wayne was in the bathroom shaving. I came in and made some small talk while I scanned the dresser, still littered with party detritus.

"Whatcha looking for, son?" Baker said.

"Oh, I thought I left a pack of cigarettes here last night," I said lamely.

"I mighta seen that," Baker said. "Did it have anything in it? Like this?" He held up the joint.

"Yeah, it did," I said.

"Is it any good?" he asked.

"Yeah, it's really good," I said.

"Well, by God, let's just see if it is," Baker said, then popped it between his lips and lit it up.

I glanced at Wayne, who had stopped shaving and was regarding us in the mirror, looking alarmed.

We had two or three hits. Then Baker walked over and flushed the rest down the toilet.

"Oh, hell," I said, mourning the loss.

"Don't be bringing that shit on the bus or it'll be my ass," Baker said. "Now let that be the last of it, goddammit."

"Yessir."

Then we got on the bus and went back to our bunks. Baker laid down and slept for twelve hours.

PART X
"ON AND ON"

(recollected)

Bill often left the band in the dark. "Just be ready," he'd say.

I would call the office to ask Betty what color suit we were going to wear on the Opry. When I could, I would visit the office and look over her shoulder at the calendar to see when and where we were playing. Bandmates would compare notes to see whether anyone had heard about a date the others hadn't.

To question any of these things was to invite a reprimand and a worsening of the situation. Monroe yelled at me when he caught me asking Betty about the calendar. "We will *always* tell you! Now, these folks is busy here, and you leave them alone!"

"Yessir."

I was trying to plan my wedding. As it turned out, I had to cut my honeymoon short after I found out we were supposed to do a TV show in Canada.

There was another time I cut a vacation to Wisconsin short and got back to Nashville to find out it was a benefit show in Greensboro, North Carolina. (I wouldn't get paid.) When I shared my calendar with Bill because Georgia was expecting our first child and I wanted to be there for the birth if possible, he didn't tell me the date we had in Alabama was to record a gospel album. Instead, again without telling me, he called the union for a bass singer to take my place. Somehow he wound up with two guys. They sang in place of Blake and me, and the album wasn't fit to release.

With a growing family and an eye to the future, I started taking college courses in my spare time. I explained to my algebra instructor, a Mr. Bob Forrester, that I played in a band, and that when it came to my knowing the schedule, my boss was definitely a "variable" that might cause some unexpected absences. He asked who I worked for, and when I told him he laughed and said he thought he knew what I meant.

"You might know my dad," he said, "Howdy Forrester."

Of course. I saw his dad almost every time we played the Opry, fiddling with Roy Acuff. Howdy had worked with Monroe in the 1940s, and I guess his son must have heard stories.

I learned not to bring any of it up with Bill, because if he thought you had found something out ahead of time and made plans, he would change it just to cross you up. And you had no right to complain.

Baker would say, "There are three ways of doing things around here. There's a right way, a wrong way, and the Monroe way. And it's my job to do things the Monroe way."

I was glad to do the job, but I always thought I could do it better if I knew what was going on. Getting through those tight spots and upset plans was something I could usually laugh about later. But now, with a second child on the way, I needed this information for daycare and doctor appointments. It wasn't funny anymore.

I had gradually worked into the music scene in Nashville, joined some jam sessions at parties and clubs around town, and caught a few recording sessions here and there. When I was asked to play a gig at the Station Inn with the Dreadful Snakes—a pickup jam with Jerry Douglas, Béla Fleck, Roland White, Blaine Sprouse, and Pat Enright—the cassette recording of it sounded so good that Béla pitched it to Rounder Records. The resulting album, *Snakes Alive!*, sold twenty-five thousand copies right out of the gate—and now I had a record I could sell at the table (and I could keep the money).

What's more, playing with those guys was so *easy*. Most of the cuts on the *Snakes* album were first or second takes. At the end of one track, if you turn up the volume you can faintly hear Blaine call out, "Damn, boys!" We were knocking them out one after another.

Bill didn't forbid band members from working side gigs. But when he heard about them, he didn't like it. And we were making great music—so he was hearing about it, and beginning to ride me for it.

I had fallen in with Enright, Mike Compton, and Alan O'Bryant, and when an opportunity arose to do a monthlong tour with Minnie Pearl and a troupe of musicians and dancers from New York City, it became the impetus to form the Nashville Bluegrass Band. They asked me to join, and I did. Georgia was worried, but it was like a fresh breeze to me.

When you're a sideman, you're walking around in someone else's dream. I was tired of being a sideman.

(archival)

The shortest distance between two points has nothing to do with the travel plans of the Blue Grass Boys. The easiest trip can be turned into an ordeal by one or two ill-conceived decisions. Even knowing what time the bus will leave or when we'll be back is a challenge—and that just doesn't fly at home with a wife who is a working mother, now with two babies. (Katherine was about eighteen months old when Michael was born. I didn't repeat the mistake of sharing the due date with Bill.)

And that part never got any better. The day I gave Bill my two weeks' notice wasn't much different from the first day I went to work for him, when he had me show up six hours before we were scheduled to leave.

The day before, we had stayed just south of Chattanooga in Dalton, Georgia. The next date was about five hours away in Sparta, North Carolina, a little mountain town (population about 1,700) up near the Virginia state line. We finished in Dalton at 2 p.m. eastern time and didn't have to be in Sparta until the next day.

What did we do? We drove straight through all the way to Sparta, which—big surprise—had no vacancies save a single motel room. In true southern fashion, everyone felt honor bound to refuse the room.

Not me. I knew I was going to quit the next day. I took the room.

Now, a week later, I am working out my notice. This will carry me to the end of the week at Bean Blossom. Before us lies McAlester, Oklahoma, on Thursday, back to Nashville to play the Opry on Friday, back out to Albuquerque on Sunday, and Bean Blossom on the following Wednesday.

That's the initial plan, anyway. However, this morning Bill says maybe we should just proceed to Albuquerque from Oklahoma. I left home last night not knowing whether I would be back on Friday, on the following Monday or Tuesday, or perhaps not until after the Bean Blossom show on Wednesday.

June 7

It's going to be quite a month. There's a trip to Wisconsin after Bean Blossom to see family, too, and all these uncertain travel plans are complicating all other plans. The Nashville Bluegrass Band plays on June 25, and I still don't know whether I'll be back home on Friday, Tuesday, Wednesday, or sometime in July.

June 10

We returned from McAlester to play the Friday night Opry—my last one with Monroe. It was Fan Fair Week in Nashville, so the Opry house was filled to capacity. As I stood watching the curtain fall, I wondered whether I'd ever be on that stage again.

That tugged at the heart. I thought of Saturday nights in my childhood, sitting on Dad's knee listening to the Opry, hearing the crackling radio hum and pop from some faraway place as Dad narrated, telling me about the music and the things to listen for.

Five years ago, when I stepped up to a mike stand with that WSM Grand Ole Opry tag on it to sing a bass lead, I felt the heat of the spotlight on my face and it nearly paralyzed me. I felt my necktie tighten around my throat.

Later, it became a dull routine, the long hours between shows crawling by, the hallways backstage filled with desperately grinning bullshitters, guys goosing one another and slapping one another on the back, hollering, forever adolescent, like a high school recess.

But now the Opry has again become a pinnacle for me to attain, perhaps someday with a band of peers.

It's going to be fun with the Nashville Bluegrass Band: Alan and Pat are top-notch singers, Mike plays Monroe's style on mandolin as well as anyone can, the rhythm feels great, and we have a fine vocal quartet. And I won't be just a sideman.

That's more or less what I told Bill: that it's been an honor to work for him, and I appreciated everything he's done for me, but it was time for me to try to make my own way. I didn't bother to say I was tired of not being able to know when or where I was going or what we were doing.

On to Albuquerque

It's my last road trip with the Blue Grass Boys. The question is whether we'll come back through Nashville before Bean Blossom. It would help me; otherwise, I'll need to arrange for someone to drive my car up there so I can continue to Wisconsin. Then it's on to Chautauqua, New York, on June 25, for my first post-Monroe show with the Nashville Bluegrass Band; back to

Milwaukee for June 30; to Hershey, Pennsylvania, for July 4; and back in Nashville on July 6 and 7; followed by a trip to Colorado to see my sister (she has cancer, it's terminal, and this may be my last chance). After that, the Nashville Bluegrass Band has a show in Canandaigua, New York, to kick off a short New England tour.

It's Hell Month, and I still have a long way to go.

THE ROAD IS CLEAR   72

(partly archival)

June 17, 1984, Bean Blossom: my last day with Bill Monroe and the Blue Grass Boys.

When I told Bill I was leaving, he didn't have much to say. But Betty told me a few days later that he was surprised, "truly rocked," she said. I suppose from his point of view I was leaving the best job in the world. And for what? Though he knew the musicians involved, no one had ever even heard of the Nashville Bluegrass Band.

There wasn't room for much sentimentality, at least not between two guys (especially if one of them is Monroe, although he could be sentimental on his own). But I did want him to know there were times and things I would miss: being part of the Opry, being in the headliner's band, watching Bill wow a crowd, and helping him drive it home.

And, maybe most of all, Bean Blossom. I think of it as the place where I first realized I could play music for a living. I wanted to be on that stage in the shade of all those tall trees, to be in front of that big crowd and hear their applause. It's where I saw my first major-league bluegrass shows.

So much great music! Impossible to choose a favorite, foolish to try, but I have two salient memories.

First would be the time I first laid eyes on that stage. It was one of those wonderful summer evenings in Indiana, when it cooled off and everything seemed to become more reasonable. After a long day of traveling from Wisconsin, my friends and I walked up to the stage area, late in the evening near the end of the show, and there was Bill Monroe and his Blue Grass Boys.

Baker was at the peak of his powers, the incredibly sweet double stops and flawless tone filling the park, the audience hushed as he played "Jerusalem Ridge."

As Bill would say, I never will forget that.

The other would be the first time I saw Ralph Stanley's band, with Keith Whitley singing lead. At the end of a long, hot afternoon, with every band trying to outdo the previous act with power trios and instrumental derring-do, breakdown after breakdown, the audience had become desensitized. They had nothing more to give.

Then Ralph came on. And here was Keith, strumming a mid-tempo as the band fell in behind him and the crowd quieted. In that marvelous, angelic voice, he began to sing "I Just Think I'll Go Away." Then the vocal trio—Keith, Ralph, and Jack Cooke—rose to the chorus, and their harmony made the air stand still and shimmer.

After that chorus, the crowd stood up and roared for the sheer beauty of it.

It's one of my most memorable musical experiences, and it was an important lesson. You don't have to play a breakdown to move an audience. As Dad said, there's power in the music.

So, on my last Sunday at Bean Blossom, on a beautiful morning with the sun dappling the forest floor, in the quiet before the big crowd showed up, Ralph Stanley's band led off the gospel program. And as their harmonies filled the park, all those memories rose in my throat.

Up the hill from the stage, the little whitewashed shack that once had been Uncle Birch's hamburger stand now stood empty. I stepped in, closed the door, and had myself a good cry.

At the close of the festival that day, Monroe, as usual, had each of the Blue Grass Boys step up and say a few parting words. This, of course, had added significance for me. I thanked all the friends I'd made there the past few years, and again I thanked Bill for the privilege of being a Blue Grass Boy. And I said I hoped it wouldn't be long before I could come back to play at Bean Blossom again.

"The road is clear," Monroe said.

It was an ambiguous response. A friend asked me, "When he said, 'The road is clear,' did he mean c'mon back, or did he mean hit it?"

I didn't know, but I thought the latter was more likely.

After the show, Baker invited me back to his room to have one for the road. He said it was a shame that I was leaving just now; we had a lot of work coming up, and it looked like it would be a pretty good summer. I was pleased by the friendly gesture, but a little surprised—there were times he'd been pretty rough on me—and there was something about it that made me wonder how long he planned to stick around.

It was the last time I would see him. He quit Bill that fall.

GRAND OLE APRÈS 73

Monroe wouldn't speak to me after I quit. I thought, and old-timers concurred, that this put me in excellent company. Hell, he didn't talk to Lester Flatt for more than twenty years. Baker had told me that was a hell of a thing to see. Back at the old Ryman Auditorium, in the days when there were just two dressing rooms, the Opry backstage was so crowded that people would stand toe-to-toe in the wings. Bill and Lester might be caught face-to-face, and neither would look at the other or say a word.

So it was to be expected. But I guess I wasn't nearly as good as Lester, because Bill only froze me out for a couple of years.

Nashville Bluegrass Band was playing a festival in Glasgow, Delaware, and we had recently acquired a 1957 GMC 4104 bus, an old Greyhound. Dull silver with blue trim, it still bore its former band's name, *The Soundmasters*, crudely painted in shaky cursive on each side of the coach.

Bill and I found ourselves standing near each other at the backstage fence, watching the bus out in the field turning around, belching huge clouds of blue smoke. (This was before the first time the engine blew.) It was a pretty humorous sight if it wasn't your bus.

I turned to Bill, who was still gazing out across the field at our Greyhound jalopy, and said, "Boss, how do you like my new bus?"

A trace of a smile passed his lips, and he nodded. I asked how he'd been. "Pretty fair," he said. I told him I thought his band was sounding good. That was about it before the bus arrived. I wished him well and got aboard.

So, the ice was broken. Years later, after I had moved back to Wisconsin, I went to Madison to see him play a show. His bus was parked out in front of the theater. Thinking I would look up my old roomy, Blake, I knocked on the door. It was Bill who answered. He was in a jocular mood.

"Looks like you coulda come up here and got a job that you could afford to buy a razor," he said of my beard. I told him I needed it, it was cold up here. "Well, what do you want?" he asked. I just thought I'd come by and say hello, I said, and asked whether Blake was around.

"Don't you want to see me?" he asked. Sure, if you have a few minutes, I said. "Well, come on then," he said, and I followed him onto the bus.

We sat there for a little while, making small talk and catching up. I don't think I ever had a friendlier conversation with him. When I got set to leave, he said, "Now if I call your name tonight, can you get up on the stage?" Sure, I said, I'd come on as quick as I could. I wouldn't want to hold up the show. "Well, alright then," he said, and we shook hands.

And sure enough, he called me up, and I played a few numbers with the Boys that night—he even called "Rocky Road Blues," knowing he could give me a bass solo. I stayed on until the end of the set and played the closing theme, "Watermelon Hanging on the Vine," as we had so many times on the Opry. And the crowd loved it, giving the local boy a big hand.

Of course, Bill knew they would. Ever the showman, he often would call a local up onstage. That could be risky, but it usually worked out just fine—because Monroe could always carry it himself, no matter what.

AT LAST, THANKS

A bus wreck in 1988 marked the end of my professional music career. It's a longer story than that; I recovered and could have continued. But honestly, with my not realizing how badly I'd been hurt, my first thought when everything stopped moving was, "This is it. I have got to find a different way to make a living."

It was a long road back, and the charity and kindnesses shown me were too many to count. I regret not having answered every card, letter, and phone call with a separate word or note of thanks. So here it is, late as hell but I hope better (thirty-four years) late than never. I'm sorry if any of the couples listed are no longer couples, but mostly I'm sorry that some of these people may not have lived long enough for me to thank them.

First, though, thanks to my wife, Georgia, who cared for two children and the house in addition to bathing me, dressing my wounds, coordinating my care, and running down all the dastardly insurers, usurers, and providers. I hope we never have enough bad luck for me to ever repay that debt.

More thanks to our dear friend and neighbor Velma Farris, who helped with the house and kids and meals and everything. (Past ninety now, she still bakes me a peach cobbler every time I'm in Nashville.) Also, her late, great husband and friend of mine, Mr. Hollie, who took up his cane and brought me a newspaper every day to look in on me while I was laid up.

And to our longtime friends and Tennessee compadres Connie and Hugues Chevalier (who were there when we came home from the hospital), Sue and Phil Gazell (Phil assembled a hospital bed and built a wheelchair ramp before I got home), Jerry Douglas (who muscled me around to appointments), Bob Mason (who made sure I got out once in awhile), and Bill Miller, who, then new in Nashville, took on a gig to drive me home from Virginia and never made a dime—and remembered me kindly years later. Also, Athlon editors George Leonard and Daryl Sanders, who boosted my new career in journalism by bringing me onto the magazine staff as soon as I was ambulatory.

Special thanks to Denise Stiff of the Keith Case agency, who handled almost all of the correspondence and passed along donations and get-well cards.

And now, for varying degrees of contributions and compassion, and certainly not in order of magnitude (you know who you are), here's everyone else in alphabetical order. If I misplaced your card or letter or memory, I'm sorry. If I misspelled your name, it may have been your penmanship. I thank you all nonetheless.

Roger Alvis
H. W. Anderson
Don and Debbie Apanovich
Robert Arbogast
Campbell Armour
Athlon Publications
Mike Auldridge
Austin Family
Robert Babcock
Viola Bagwell
Debbie Baker
Willie and Darlene Barker
Larry Bazinet
Alfred Beaner
Ray Beasley and family
William Belfield
Bev and Kristina at Little House
    Graphics
Bluegrass Unlimited magazine
Ginger Boatwright
Howard Bonner
Roy Book Binder
Boston Bluegrass Union
Chris and Dixie Bozung
Fletcher Bright
Riece Brown

John Cabaniss
Dave Campbell
Keith Case
David Chancellor
Leonard Choate
Mike Compton
Connecticut Friends of Bluegrass
Wilma Lee Cooper
Roger Corbin
Nigle and Tom Cormen
Donald Cossitt
Charles Coyle
Wanda Dalton
Louise Davidson
Lee Michael Dempsey
J. Dennis
Doug Dillard
Michael D. Dingus
Tim Donovan
Mike and Jan Dowling
Down Home, Johnson City,
    Tennessee
D. L. Drake
Liz Duncan
Stuart Duncan
W. W. Edwards Jr.

Julian Elliott
Sydney and Jane Ellis
Tom Ellis
D. Engstrom
Pat Enright
Mark Fenster
Clark and Gail Ferguson
Ken and Jane Finkel
Alvin C. Floen
Becky Floyd
Edward Forshee
David Freeman, County Sales
Frets magazine
Ruth Gibson
Priscilla Gillespie
Bob and Dorothy Gillim
Rosalie Goldstein
Cathy Goode
Cathy Goodman
J. T. Gray
The Greers (of Idaho)
Vicki and Galen Greve
Pieter Groenveld
Susan Hammond
John Hartford
Bill Hartten
J. L. Hathcock
George Healy
Travis Holloway
Steve Houston
James R. Howard
Glenn and Carol Huffer
Mary Jackson
Horace and Hattie Jernigan
Richard and Trish Johnston
Elbert Jones
Rich Kalikow

Louis Kaplan
KCLC-FM, Saint Charles, Missouri
KCSM, San Mateo, California
Shirley Kennard
Pete Kennedy
Jean Kessinger
Merle and Joyce Kilby
Shu Kimura
Kay Knight
Paul Kovac
KPFK, Canoga Park, California
Alison Krauss and Union Station
Rich Krohn
Pete and Kitty Kuykendall
Jane Lancaster
Bob "Hobo" Larkin
Roz and Howard Larman
Ruby Larrigan
Meg Larson
Lee Michael Lemzey
Thomas Lesh
Wayne and Sue Lewis
Chuck and Denise Little
Melvin Little
Vernon and Virginia Long
Lost & Found
Peter Ludé
Jimmy Martin
Maura McConnell
Victoria McMullen
Jim McPike
Richard J. McVey
Walt Michael
Kristy Miller/Bill Harrell and the
    Virginians
Miss Judy
Bill Monroe

Lynn Morris

James Nelson

Lillian K. Nelson

Pete and Janis Nelson

Peter Nelson

David O'Brien

Alan O'Bryant

Maura O'Connell

Gary and Linda Oelze

Art Parker

Fred and Mary Lou Pement

J. B. Penn

Ron Pensky

Daniel J. Penzer

Al Perkins

Sam Perkins

Vicki Perry Douglas

Nina and Burt Philp

Al and Barb Plempel

Pat and Gene Polewski

Anna Pontius

Charlie and Bobbie Price

Julie Price

Sherry Price-Wiese and family

Jim Queen

Joyce and Michael Reed

Pete and Arlene Reiniger

Noel Rendleman

Chet Rhodes

Kenneth and Emily Ritchie

Ted Robinette

David Robinson

Robert Rogers

Steve Rosenstein

Rounder Records: Ken Irwin,
    Marian Leighton Levy, Bill
    Nowlin

Peter Rowan

Japhy Ryder

Dave Samuelson

Deb Sander

Susan Sandstrom

Mark Schatz

Jeff R. Scofield

Scopp Family

Annette Shaw

G. Simko

Chris and Tom Skinker

Fred Skolnick

Brian Smith

Connie Smith

Daryl Smith

Bill Stamper

Coleen Stephens

Larry and Mary Stephens

Elsie S. Stewart

Steven Stielstra

Sue Suasti

Carolyn Suchecki

Michael P. Swanson

Bill and Edith Sykes

Pudge Tarbett at the Birchmere

Don and Deanna Taylor

Joe Terry

Carl and Sophie Tipton

Traci Todd

Linda Toivainen

Bill and Janie Tomerlin

Lewis M. Umbarger

Frances Ann Veal

Bill Vernon

Butch and Kathy Waller

WAMU, Washington, DC

Tony Washburn

Doc Watson
George and Sarah Watson
Jim and Dorothy Webb
Bob Webster
Glynelle Wells
Jane Wells
Buck, Cheryl, and Sharon White
Carlton Whitehead
James Whitt
WHRB, Cambridge, Massachusetts
Charles F. Wilky
Blake Williams

Andrea Willis
Charlie and Lou Wilson
Winnipeg Folk Festival
Ben Winship
James P. Winship
Marty and Myrna Wolfe
Kenneth Dale Wood
S. W. Wood
WPAY, Portsmouth, Ohio
Paula and Steve Zeithin
Rich Ziven

Adler, Thomas A. *Bean Blossom: The Brown County Jamboree and Bill Monroe's Bluegrass Festivals*. Urbana: University of Illinois Press, 2011.

Ewing, Tom. *Bill Monroe: The Life and Music of the Blue Grass Man*. Urbana: University of Illinois Press, 2018.

———, ed. *The Bill Monroe Reader*. Urbana: University of Illinois Press, 2000.

Feldman, Jay. "Bluegrass Baseball: Barnstorming Band and Ball Club, Bill Monroe, Other Musicians Sponsored Teams in 1930–40s." *Baseball Research Journal*, 1984. https://sabr.org/journals/1984-baseball-research-journal.

Peva, Jim. *Bean Blossom: Its People and Its Music*. Conshohocken: Infinity, 2006.

Rinzler, Ralph. "Bill Monroe: The Daddy of Blue Grass Music," *Sing Out!* 13 (February–March 1963): 5–8.

———. "Bill Monroe." In *Stars of Country Music: Uncle Dave Macon to Johnny Rodriguez*, edited by Bill C. Malone and Judith McCulloh, 202–21. Urbana: University of Illinois Press, 1975.

———. *Blue Grass Instrumentals*. Decca DL 74601, 1965, LP, liner notes (uncredited).

———. *The High, Lonesome Sound of Bill Monroe and His Bluegrass Boys*, Decca DL 74780, 1966, LP, liner notes.

Rooney, James. *Bossmen: Bill Monroe & Muddy Waters*. New York: Da Capo Press, 1991.

Rosenberg, Neil V., comp. *Bill Monroe and His Blue Grass Boys: An Illustrated Discography*. Nashville: Country Music Foundation Press, 1974.

———. *Bluegrass: A History*. Urbana: University of Illinois Press, 2005.

———. *Bluegrass Generation: A Memoir*. Urbana: University of Illinois Press, 2018.

———. *The Music of Bill Monroe*. Urbana: University of Illinois Press, 2007.

Rosenberg, Neil V., and Charles K. Wolfe. *The Music of Bill Monroe*. Urbana: University of Illinois Press, 2007.

Rumble, John W. "Bill Monroe." In *The Encyclopedia of Country Music*, 2nd ed., comp. Country Music Hall of Fame and Museum, ed. Paul Kingsbury, Michael McCall, and John W. Rumble. New York: Oxford University Press, 2012.

Smith, Richard D. *Can't You Hear Me Callin'*. Boston: Little, Brown, 2000.

Wolfe, Charles K. *Classic Country: Legends of Country Music*. New York: Routledge, 2001.

———. *A Good-Natured Riot: The Birth of the Grand Ole Opry*. Nashville: Country Music Foundation Press and Vanderbilt University Press, 1999.
———. *Kentucky Country: Folk and Country Music of Kentucky*. Lexington: University Press of Kentucky, 1996.
———. *The Music of Bill Monroe*/Neil V. Rosenberg and Charles K. Wolfe. Urbana: University of Illinois Press.

Acuff, Roy, 10, 11, 62, 179
Adler, Thomas A., xii, 13, 193, 203
album concession, 38, 60, 62, 88, 119–20, 141–42
Amen Corner, 38, 117
Appalachia, 121, 151, 173
Astro Motel, 27, 35
audition, 15–17
Avery Fisher Hall, 64

Bain, Aly, 102
Baker, Kenny: advice on lodging, 27; advice regarding Monroe, 64, 65; arrival in Honolulu, 94; banana prank, 76–77; on baseball, 147; bass preference, 81; bidding farewell, 185; busts me for pot, 175–76; at cards, 109–12; caught with beer, 57, 58; celebrating Monroe's birthday, 145–46; characterized by Douglas Green, 22; in DC, 47–48; declaring fiddle at Canadian customs, 104; demeanor, 23; ears, 23; "Flop," 23; "Greatest Fiddle Player," 22, 118; hires me to sell records, 142; home plans, 116; on Hot Rize, 69; in Ireland, 157–58; literacy, 23; musical style, 22–23, 184; at my audition, 16; onstage antics, 61–62, 131; personal profile, 22–23; photos, 87, 89–91, 93–94; pricing rooms, 74; pro-union views, 150; recalling Flatt feud, 185; religious views, 173; scolding me, 55, 176, 184; with Tommy Jarrell, 110; warns show host about Monroe's health, 86; wartime service, 22; wisecracks, 47, 53, 161; in Wyoming snow storm, 74

Bakker, Jim and Tammy Faye, 172–73
baseball, 6, 146–49
bass (borrowed), 56–57, 102
Bean Blossom (festival), xii; 22; Birch Monroe's role, 39–40; calling cattle, 119; description of grounds, 37–38; hippy audience, 174; international audience, 116–17; my last day, 183–84; photos, 87–89, 91–93, 98, 116–17; relieved of concession duty, 141–42; stove incident, 125–26
Bean Blossom '79 (live album), 54, 81
Bean Blossom (live double album), 141–42
beer, Monroe's views, 4, 57–58, 141, 148
Belfast, Northern Ireland, 159–60
Berline, Byron, 11, 145
Bill Monroe's Uncle Pen (album), 81
Blake, Norman, 11, 81–82
Blankenship, Junior, 152
Blue Grass Boys: baseball, 147; bass preferences, 81; books by, xii; bus quarters, 52; celebrating Monroe's birthday in Louisville, 144–46; chasing heckler, 169–70; at customs, 102–3; in DC, 47; dress, 15; duties, 118, former, 11; hazing, 26, 29, 32, 33; hung over, 59–60; influential, 7; in Ireland, 157; in Israel, 163–65; in Lake Tahoe, 113; on Mule Day, 128–29; my debut, 20; 1982 World's Fair, 129–31; in Nova Scotia, 140; personal profiles, 21–26; photos, 87, 89, 91, 93–94; reviewed in Washington Post, 49; shoes, 41–42; stance, 16; used for recording, 162; at the Watergate, 50; at the White House, 48

Bluegrass Music Festival of the United States, 69

Blue Grass Quartet: photo, 89; recording, 136

Bridgewater, Nova Scotia, 139–41

Brown County, Indiana, 37–38

Brown County Jamboree, 37, 125

bus descriptions, 51–52, 108, 113, 126

Bush, Sam, 70, 171–72, 175

Byrd, Sen. Robert, "Fiddling Senator," 63

Caesars Palace, 113–14

Canadian customs, 103–4

Carter, Jimmy, 43, 47–49, 63–64; photo, 88, 130

Cash, Johnny, 47–48

Cathedral Caverns, 135–36

Centers, Roy Lee, 152

Chatom, Alabama, 31–34, 173

Clements, Vassar, 11, 175, 69

Coeburn, Virginia, 149

Columbia, Tennessee: Mule Day, 128; photo, 93

Compton, Mike, 116, 180

Conn, Mervyn, 157, 160–61

Cooke, Jack, 151, 154, 184

Cork, Ireland, 157–59

Country Music Hall of Fame and Museum, xi, 3, 145, 161

Crowe, J. D., 37, 69, 98

Cumberland Gap, 77

Davis, Randy, 15, 21, 25, 81

Denver, Colorado, 12, 15, 51

Dickerson Pike, 19, 27, 35

Donald (bus driver), 75, 77–78

Douglas, Jerry, 69, 70, 118, 180, 187

Dreadful Snakes, 180

Duffey, John, 72–73

Duvall, Robert, 9

Dylan, Bob, 3, 11

East Chicago, Indiana, 5

Enright, Pat, 135, 180

Ewing, Tom, xii, xiii

Father of Blue Grass Music, 3, 15, 19, 43, 161. *See* Monroe, Bill

Feldman, Jay, xiii, 147

felt hats, 42

Flatt, Lester: banjo requirements, 26; at Bean Blossom, 37; compared to Charlie Waller, 72; feud with Monroe, 185; hometown, 25; memorial, 131; with Monroe, 5; on Opry, 6; at poker, 111

Flatt and Scruggs, 5–7, 38, 149

Fleck, Béla, 12, 27, 180

Ford's Theatre, 42, 47–50

Fowler, Bob, 23

Frankfurt, Germany, 160

Galax, Virginia, 109, 122

Georgia Barbecue, 63

Gibson, 10, 28, 104, 145

gospel album, 135–36, 179

Grand Ole Opry, 3; audience reaction to Monroe, 5; backstage at Ryman Auditorium, 185; backstage photos, 91–92; Blue Grass Boy rehearsals, 28; Flatt and Scruggs membership, 5–6; Greenbriar Boys appearance, 7; listening in Wisconsin, 10; my last show, 182; origin, 5; prominence, 5; shuns Elvis Presley, 62

Green, Douglas ("Ranger Doug"), 22, 89

Greenbriar Boys, 3, 7

Guarnerius violin, 22, 104

Haynes, Walter, 53

Henes-Hembree, Georgia: acknowledged, xiii; declines trip to Israel, 163; expecting, 135; goes into labor, 137; meets Jerry Douglas's wife Vicki, 70; move to Colorado and back, 12; photos, 87, 91; proposal, 56; reaction to audition, 17; thanked, 187; worried about new band, 180

Hills of Home festival, 149–51

hippies, at Bean Blossom, 174

Honolulu, Hawai'i: photo, 94, 126–28

Huffmaster, Raymond, 15–16

Huskey, "Junior," 11

Huskey, Roy, 81

Hutchens, Doug, 144–45

International Festival of Country Music (Wembley), 58, 157

Ireland, 159–60
Israel, 163–65

Jackson, Kentucky, 152
Japanese tourists at Bean Blossom, 116–17
Jarrell, Tommy, 109–10, 122
Jenkins, Kentucky, 22, 147, 150
Jim & Jesse. *See* McReynolds
job offer, 18
Johnson, Lloyd, 137–38
Jordan River, 96, 164

Kentucky, Eastern, 124, 152
Kentucky Fried Chicken, 8, 69, 144
Knowlton, Bill, 86
Knoxville International Energy Exposition (Knoxville World's Fair), 129–30
Krenke, Bob, 17

La Bella, Julia, 127, 129, 142
Landmark Theater, Syracuse, New York, 86
last day, 183–85
Lewis, Wayne: allegiance to South, 25; bass preference, 81; at Breathitt County Coliseum, 153; at cards, 111–12; celebrates Monroe birthday, 144; charms state trooper, 25; chasing heckler, 169; collects Monroe's pay, 24; declares at Canadian customs, 104; as driver, 25; escorts ill Monroe from stage, 140; guides bus up Cumberland Gap, 77–78; hat advice, 42; helps me get to airport, 137; home plans, 116; ill in Lake Tahoe, 114; on illiterate fans, 120; Israel tour, 97, 163; kidding bus driver, 60; leader onstage, 25; needling me, 40; needling Monroe, 112–13; nickname ("Durango"), 25; personal profile, 23–24; photos, 87, 89, 94, 97; placates Johnny Paycheck, 127; relieves bus driver, 73–74; remark at Chatom, 34; remark at Moose Lodge, 109; scolding onstage, 62; sends help to Monroe, 52; southern expressions, 25; at World's Fair, 131
Lincoln Center, New York City, 64
Lloyd Loar mandolin, 28, 104
Lockwood Park, Alabama, 32

London, England, 54, 58, 157
Louisville, Kentucky, 69, 144
lyrics, morbid, 121–22

Macon, Uncle Dave, 61
Malone, Bill, 7
Many, Louisiana, 61
Martha White, 6
Martin, Jimmy, 5, 11, 15, 37, 98
Master of Bluegrass, 26, 81–84
McClure, Virginia, 149–51
McInturff, Betty, 138, 142, 179, 183
McReynolds, Jim and Jesse, 25, 33, 37, 98, 157
Metropole Hotel, Cork, Ireland, 158
Milwaukee Brewers, 148–49
Missouri State Fair, 120
Monroe, Bertha, 4
Monroe, Bill: accepts patriarchal role, 7; acoustic set in Pittsburgh, 169; angered, 41; annoyed by clown, 149; on baseball, 146–49; birthday ceremony in Louisville, 144–46; brothers, 4, 5, 39; business ineptitude, 9; calling cattle, 119; at cards, 111–12; Cathedral Caverns recording, 135–36; chasing heckler, 169–70; childhood, 4; confirms job, 28; declares mandolin at Canadian customs, 104; dining preferences, 52–54; on drunkenness, 4; on Elvis Presley, 62; encore in Zürich, 160–62; in England and Ireland, 157–58; feats of strength, 4; at Ford's Theatre, 47, 49–50; in Galax, Virginia, 109–10; gift to my newborn, 138; hangover hazing, 59–60; on hippies at Bean Blossom, 174–75; hires Blake Williams, 26; ill in Nova Scotia, 139–40; influence, 8; intensity, 3, 50; Israel tour, 163–65; "I will never change," 4; in Jackson, Kentucky, 152–54; keeping Flatt and Scruggs off Opry, 5; kindness, 36; lexicon, 29; loathes beer, 57–59; loses parents, 4; magical deeds, 170–72; *Master of Bluegrass* album, 81; monitoring Johnny Paycheck, 127–28; on Mule Day, 128–29; musical demands, 8; music instruction, 8; at my audition, 15–17;

Monroe, Bill (*continued*): my first show, 19–20; "My Last Days on Earth," 81–83; mystified by my acquaintances, 63–65; needles me onstage, 33–34; offers job, 18–19; Opry debut, 5; original bluegrass band, 5; parting words, 184; pays band in coins, 6; with Pendleton Vandiver ("Uncle Pen"), 4; personal profile, 3–9; photos, 87, 89–91, 93–97; on poor turnout, 61; poor vision, 4; post-op touring, 84–86, 105, 123; pricing rooms, 114; on progressive bluegrass, 69; proud of reading, 4; on punctuality, 55; punitive rhythm, 8; Ralph Rinzler interview, 7; rapid recovery, 141; reacts to my resignation, 183; recalled by Don Reno, 6; reconciliation, 185–86; relieves me of record duty, 141–42; remarks on borrowed bass, 56–57; reputation as stern, 6; rise to stardom, 5; "school of music," 162; seeking souvenir rocks, 106; showmanship, 8, 160–62, 186; shuns *Will the Circle Be Unbroken* record project, 11; snubs Robert Duvall, 9; sparring with Wayne Lewis, 112–13; starts festival at Bean Blossom, 37–38; stove trouble at Bean Blossom, 125–26; taciturn demeanor, 7; versus John Duffey, 72–74; waning popularity, 5; West Coast touring, 101–2; at White House, 48; witholds itinerary, 56, 107, 108, 179–80; work in East Chicago, Indiana, 5; at World's Fair, 129–31
Monroe, Birch, 4–5, 38–40, 92, 125, 131–32
Monroe, Carolyn, 19
Monroe, Charlie, 4, 5, 39
Monroe, James, 19, 26, 62, 85, 143
Monroe Doctrine, 11–12, 15, 51
Monroe Enterprises, 19, 109, 123, 126
Mule Day parade, 128–29; photo, 93

Nashville, Tennessee: Fan Fair, 182; housing, 35; joining music scene, 180; Monroe's baseball team, 147; musicians union, 112; my first days, 27; WSM Grand Ole Opry, 5

Nashville Bluegrass Band, 180, 182–83, 185
NBC production crew, 49–50
New Grass Revival, 25, 69
New York City, 64–65
New York Times (Kenny Baker obituary), 22

O'Brien, Tim, 69
O'Bryant, Alan, 27, 180
Osborne Brothers, (*Bobby and Sonny*), 37, 98

Parton, Dolly, 47–49
Pasadena, California, 101–2
Paycheck, Johnny, 126–28
Peva, Ailene, 117
Peva, Jim, xii
Pittsburgh, Pennsylvania, 169
Pocatello, Idaho, 73–74
Poitín, 159–60
Presley, Elvis, 5, 8, 62
Prestige, Dee Dee (Diana Christian, neé Delores Bacon), 164
PTL Club, 172–73
Pushkin, Jon, 15–18

Rainwater, Cedric (Howard Watts), 5, 147
Reagan, Ronald, 130
Red Knuckles and the Trailblazers, 69
Reno, Don, 6, 37, 147
resignation, 181–83
Rinzler, Ralph, xii, 3–4, 6–7, 9, 11, 75
Robins, Butch: bass preference, 81; BC Powders, 70; on *Bean Blossom '79*, 54; beer theory, 57; beseeched by Monroe, 85; catching Monroe's fastball, 146; challenges Monroe, 59; declares banjo at Canadian customs, 104; existential question, 71; gloves/banana prank, 76–77; help with orientation, 25; home plans, 116; ill in Lake Tahoe, 114; on Monroe instrumentals, 26; at my audition, 16–17; on my first gig, 20; nicknames Wayne Lewis, 24; observes my evolving attitude, 76; personal profile, 25–26; previous bands, 25; razzed by Monroe, 59; reacts to Monroe apology,

86; saves Monroe from London taxi, 54; singing trio with Monroe, John Duffey, 73; track deleted on "Fair Play," 82; wardrobe tips, 42; at White House, 48

Rooney, James (Jim), xii, 9

Rosenberg, Neil V., xii, 7

Rosine, Kentucky, 4, 55, 131

Rounder Records, 69, 180

Rowan, Peter, 8, 11, 39, 95, 157, 174–75

Rumble, John, xi, xii

Ruritan Club hall, Galax, Virginia, 109, 122

Savino, 117–18

Scruggs, Earl, 5, 11, 170

Scruggs, Louise, 7

Secret Service, 130

Seeger, Mike, 3

selling records, 36, 60, 62, 119–20, 141–42

shoes (polishing techniques): importance in South, 41; Monroe inspection, 42

Silver Eagle bus, 51, 74–75, 77, 106–7, 123

Sing Out! magazine, 6

Sizemore, Charlie, 154

Skaggs, Ricky, 34, 69–71, 131

Slop. *Aee* beer

Smithsonian, 3, 75

South Shore Exhibition, Bridgewater, Nova Scotia, 140

split-string tuning, 82

Stanley, Carter, 124, 151–53

Stanley, Ralph, 37, 98, 152–53, 184

Stanley Brothers (Carter and Ralph), 124, 149, 151, 153, 170

Station Inn, 70, 180

Story, Carl, 37, 98

Strauss, Richard, 83

Taylor, Red, 145

tent shows, 146

Terry, Gordon, 145–46

Three-Way Motel, Coeburn, Virginia, 149

Tiberias, Israel, 164

Tombstone Junction, 3

Tommy Hunter Show, 56

2001: A Space Odyssey, 83

University of Illinois Press, xiii

Val, Joe, 116

Vandiver, Pendleton, 4

Vega, Chevy, 34, 76–77

Walkway of the States, 90, 106

Washington, DC, 47, 50, 72, 75

Washington Post, 48–49

Watergate Hotel, 43, 47, 49–50

Watson, Doc, 11, 63

Watts, Howard (Cedric Rainwater), 5, 147

Wembley country music festival (International Festival of Country Music), 58, 157

Wernick, Peter (Dr. Banjo), 69–70

West Coast, 11, 56, 59, 101–4

Western Wall, 97, 164

Whitaker, Charlie, 123–24, 126, 143

White, Buck, 40, 69

White, L. E., 142–43

White House, 42–43, 48, 63–64, 73, 75, 88

Whitley, Keith, 184

Williams, Blake: at Birch Monroe's funeral, 132; with Bobby Smith, 25; Cathedral Caverns recording, 136; celebrating Monroe birthday in Louisville, 144; clown story, 149; disarming sideman, 162; on Heritage USA, 172; hometown, 25; humor, 25; in Ireland, 159; Israel tour, 163; with James Monroe, 26; jukebox judgment, 124; kindness, 25; learning *Master of Bluegrass* instrumentals, 26; with Lester Flatt, 25; local DJ, 25; on McClure, 150; on Missouri, 120; personal profile, 25–26, 35; photos, 89, 91, 92, 94; playing breakdowns, 26; on progressive bluegrass, 174; regarding my Vega, 35, 139; on Robert Duvall, 9; on southern dialects, 26; stove incident, 125, 129; at World's Fair, 131; in Zürich, 161

Williams, Hank Jr., 143, 44

Will the Circle Be Unbroken (album), 11

Wisconsin: attitudes about beer, 58; country music, 37; meeting Joe Clark, 83; my early career, 10–12; photo, 87; visiting Monroe in Madison, 186

Wise, Chubby, 5, 147

Wiseman, Mac, 163

Wolfe, Charles K., xii

Wood, A. L. 123

WSM, 5, 140, 182

Yankee Devil's Dictionary, 29–30

Ziven, Rich, 65, 91, 108–10

MUSICAL COMPOSITIONS

"A Beautiful Life," 16

"Also Sprach Zarathustra," 83

"Always Late," 69

"Banks of the Ohio," 121

"Blue Moon of Kentucky," 8, 49–50, 62, 131

"Carroll County Blues," 40

"Cheyenne," 83

"Come Hither to Go Yonder," 81

"Coming Down from Boston," 40

"Down with the Old Canoe," 121

"Dueling Banjos" ("Feudin' Banjos"), 11

"Evening Prayer Blues," 81

"Flop-Eared Mule," 23

"Goodbye Old Pal," 122, 128

"He Will Set Your Fields on Fire," 122

"How Great Thou Art," 122

"I Just Think I'll Go Away," 124, 184

"Jerusalem Ridge," 22, 158, 164, 184

"Letter Edged in Black," 121

"Little Georgia Rose," 140

"Little Girl and the Dreadful Snake, The"
   121

"Little Rosewood Casket," 121

"Lochwood," 81

"Long Black Veil," 122

"Memories of Mother and Dad," 121

"Molly and Tenbrooks," 128

"Mother's Not Dead (She's Only Sleeping)," 121, 153

"Mr. Bojangles," 11

"Muleskinner Blues," 13, 128

"My Last Days on Earth," 82–83

"Old Blue," 122

"Old Gray Mare Came Tearing Out of the Wilderness, The" 128

"Old Joe Clark," 72

"Ole Ebenezer Scrooge," 81, 83

"Philadelphia Lawyer," 122

"Pretty Polly," 121

"Put My Little Shoes Away," 121

"Rawhide," 117, 145

"Road to Columbus," 16

"Rocky Road Blues," 186

"Roll in My Sweet Baby's Arms," 154

"Secret of the Waterfall," 122

"Stanleys Will Sing Again, The" 153

"That's All Right Mama," 62

"This World Is Not My Home," 122

"Turkey in the Straw," 175

"Uncle Pen," 4, 145

"Watermelon Hanging on the Vine," 186

"Were You There," 10

"Wheel Hoss," 128

"Will the Circle Be Unbroken," 121

"Wreck of the Old 97," 121

MARK HEMBREE is a bassist, vocalist, writer, and editor. From 1979 to 1984, Hembree worked for Bill Monroe as a Blue Grass Boy. He cofounded the Nashville Bluegrass Band in 1984 and was a member until 1988.

MUSIC IN AMERICAN LIFE

Only a Miner: Studies in Recorded Coal-Mining Songs   *Archie Green*

Great Day Coming: Folk Music and the American Left   *R. Serge Denisoff*

John Philip Sousa: A Descriptive Catalog of His Works   *Paul E. Bierley*

The Hell-Bound Train: A Cowboy Songbook   *Glenn Ohrlin*

Oh, Didn't He Ramble: The Life Story of Lee Collins, as Told to Mary
    Collins   *Edited by Frank J. Gillis and John W. Miner*

American Labor Songs of the Nineteenth Century   *Philip S. Foner*

Stars of Country Music: Uncle Dave Macon to Johnny Rodriguez
    Edited by Bill C. Malone and Judith McCulloh

Git Along, Little Dogies: Songs and Songmakers of the American West
    John I. White

A Texas-Mexican *Cancionero*: Folksongs of the Lower Border   *Américo Paredes*

San Antonio Rose: The Life and Music of Bob Wills   *Charles R. Townsend*

Early Downhome Blues: A Musical and Cultural Analysis   *Jeff Todd Titon*

An Ives Celebration: Papers and Panels of the Charles Ives Centennial Festival-
    Conference   *Edited by H. Wiley Hitchcock and Vivian Perlis*

Sinful Tunes and Spirituals: Black Folk Music to the Civil War   *Dena J. Epstein*

Joe Scott, the Woodsman-Songmaker   *Edward D. Ives*

Jimmie Rodgers: The Life and Times of America's Blue Yodeler   *Nolan Porterfield*

Early American Music Engraving and Printing: A History of Music Publishing
    in America from 1787 to 1825, with Commentary on Earlier and Later
    Practices   *Richard J. Wolfe*

Sing a Sad Song: The Life of Hank Williams   *Roger M. Williams*

Long Steel Rail: The Railroad in American Folksong   *Norm Cohen*

Resources of American Music History: A Directory of Source Materials from
    Colonial Times to World War II   *D. W. Krummel, Jean Geil, Doris J. Dyen,
    and Deane L. Root*

Tenement Songs: The Popular Music of the Jewish Immigrants   *Mark Slobin*

Ozark Folksongs   *Vance Randolph; edited and abridged by Norm Cohen*

Oscar Sonneck and American Music   *Edited by William Lichtenwanger*

Bluegrass Breakdown: The Making of the Old Southern Sound   *Robert Cantwell*

Bluegrass: A History   *Neil V. Rosenberg*

Music at the White House: A History of the American Spirit   *Elise K. Kirk*

Red River Blues: The Blues Tradition in the Southeast   *Bruce Bastin*

Good Friends and Bad Enemies: Robert Winslow Gordon and the Study of
    American Folksong   *Debora Kodish*

Fiddlin' Georgia Crazy: Fiddlin' John Carson, His Real World, and the World
    of His Songs   *Gene Wiggins*

America's Music: From the Pilgrims to the Present (rev. 3d ed.)   *Gilbert Chase*

Secular Music in Colonial Annapolis: The Tuesday Club, 1745–56   *John Barry Talley*

Bibliographical Handbook of American Music   *D. W. Krummel*

Goin' to Kansas City   *Nathan W. Pearson Jr.*

"Susanna," "Jeanie," and "The Old Folks at Home": The Songs of Stephen C. Foster from His Time to Ours (2d ed.)   *William W. Austin*

Songprints: The Musical Experience of Five Shoshone Women   *Judith Vander*

"Happy in the Service of the Lord": Afro-American Gospel Quartets in Memphis   *Kip Lornell*

Paul Hindemith in the United States   *Luther Noss*

"My Song Is My Weapon": People's Songs, American Communism, and the Politics of Culture, 1930–50   *Robbie Lieberman*

Chosen Voices: The Story of the American Cantorate   *Mark Slobin*

Theodore Thomas: America's Conductor and Builder of Orchestras, 1835–1905   *Ezra Schabas*

"The Whorehouse Bells Were Ringing" and Other Songs Cowboys Sing   *Collected and edited by Guy Logsdon*

Crazeology: The Autobiography of a Chicago Jazzman   *Bud Freeman, as told to Robert Wolf*

Discoursing Sweet Music: Brass Bands and Community Life in Turn-of-the-Century Pennsylvania   *Kenneth Kreitner*

Mormonism and Music: A History   *Michael Hicks*

Voices of the Jazz Age: Profiles of Eight Vintage Jazzmen   *Chip Deffaa*

Pickin' on Peachtree: A History of Country Music in Atlanta, Georgia   *Wayne W. Daniel*

Bitter Music: Collected Journals, Essays, Introductions, and Librettos   *Harry Partch; edited by Thomas McGeary*

Ethnic Music on Records: A Discography of Ethnic Recordings Produced in the United States, 1893 to 1942   *Richard K. Spottswood*

Downhome Blues Lyrics: An Anthology from the Post–World War II Era   *Jeff Todd Titon*

Ellington: The Early Years   *Mark Tucker*

Chicago Soul   *Robert Pruter*

That Half-Barbaric Twang: The Banjo in American Popular Culture   *Karen Linn*

Hot Man: The Life of Art Hodes   *Art Hodes and Chadwick Hansen*

The Erotic Muse: American Bawdy Songs (2d ed.)   *Ed Cray*

Barrio Rhythm: Mexican American Music in Los Angeles   *Steven Loza*

The Creation of Jazz: Music, Race, and Culture in Urban America   *Burton W. Peretti*

Charles Martin Loeffler: A Life Apart in Music   *Ellen Knight*

Club Date Musicians: Playing the New York Party Circuit   *Bruce A. MacLeod*

Opera on the Road: Traveling Opera Troupes in the United States, 1825–60   *Katherine K. Preston*

The Stonemans: An Appalachian Family and the Music That Shaped Their Lives   *Ivan M. Tribe*

Transforming Tradition: Folk Music Revivals Examined   *Edited by Neil V. Rosenberg*

The Crooked Stovepipe: Athapaskan Fiddle Music and Square Dancing in Northeast Alaska and Northwest Canada   *Craig Mishler*

Traveling the High Way Home: Ralph Stanley and the World of Traditional
    Bluegrass Music   *John Wright*
Carl Ruggles: Composer, Painter, and Storyteller   *Marilyn Ziffrin*
Never without a Song: The Years and Songs of Jennie Devlin, 1865–1952
    Katharine D. Newman
The Hank Snow Story   *Hank Snow, with Jack Ownbey and Bob Burris*
Milton Brown and the Founding of Western Swing   *Cary Ginell, with special
    assistance from Roy Lee Brown*
Santiago de Murcia's "Códice Saldívar No. 4": A Treasury of Secular Guitar Music
    from Baroque Mexico   *Craig H. Russell*
The Sound of the Dove: Singing in Appalachian Primitive Baptist
    Churches   *Beverly Bush Patterson*
Heartland Excursions: Ethnomusicological Reflections on Schools of Music
    Bruno Nettl
Doowop: The Chicago Scene   *Robert Pruter*
Blue Rhythms: Six Lives in Rhythm and Blues   *Chip Deffaa*
Shoshone Ghost Dance Religion: Poetry Songs and Great Basin Context
    Judith Vander
Go Cat Go! Rockabilly Music and Its Makers   *Craig Morrison*
'Twas Only an Irishman's Dream: The Image of Ireland and the Irish in American
    Popular Song Lyrics, 1800–1920   *William H. A. Williams*
Democracy at the Opera: Music, Theater, and Culture in New York City,
    1815–60   *Karen Ahlquist*
Fred Waring and the Pennsylvanians   *Virginia Waring*
Woody, Cisco, and Me: Seamen Three in the Merchant Marine   *Jim Longhi*
Behind the Burnt Cork Mask: Early Blackface Minstrelsy and Antebellum American
    Popular Culture   *William J. Mahar*
Going to Cincinnati: A History of the Blues in the Queen City   *Steven C. Tracy*
Pistol Packin' Mama: Aunt Molly Jackson and the Politics of Folksong
    Shelly Romalis
Sixties Rock: Garage, Psychedelic, and Other Satisfactions   *Michael Hicks*
The Late Great Johnny Ace and the Transition from R&B to Rock 'n' Roll
    James M. Salem
Tito Puente and the Making of Latin Music   *Steven Loza*
Juilliard: A History   *Andrea Olmstead*
Understanding Charles Seeger, Pioneer in American Musicology
    Edited by Bell Yung and Helen Rees
Mountains of Music: West Virginia Traditional Music from *Goldenseal*
    Edited by John Lilly
Alice Tully: An Intimate Portrait   *Albert Fuller*
A Blues Life   *Henry Townsend, as told to Bill Greensmith*
Long Steel Rail: The Railroad in American Folksong (2d ed.)   *Norm Cohen*
The Golden Age of Gospel   *Text by Horace Clarence Boyer;
    photography by Lloyd Yearwood*
Aaron Copland: The Life and Work of an Uncommon Man   *Howard Pollack*

Louis Moreau Gottschalk   *S. Frederick Starr*
Race, Rock, and Elvis   *Michael T. Bertrand*
Theremin: Ether Music and Espionage   *Albert Glinsky*
Poetry and Violence: The Ballad Tradition of Mexico's Costa Chica
    John H. McDowell
The Bill Monroe Reader   *Edited by Tom Ewing*
Music in Lubavitcher Life   *Ellen Koskoff*
Zarzuela: Spanish Operetta, American Stage   *Janet L. Sturman*
Bluegrass Odyssey: A Documentary in Pictures and Words, 1966–86
    Carl Fleischhauer and Neil V. Rosenberg
That Old-Time Rock & Roll: A Chronicle of an Era, 1954–63   *Richard Aquila*
Labor's Troubadour   *Joe Glazer*
American Opera   *Elise K. Kirk*
Don't Get above Your Raisin': Country Music and the Southern Working
    Class   *Bill C. Malone*
John Alden Carpenter: A Chicago Composer   *Howard Pollack*
Heartbeat of the People: Music and Dance of the Northern Pow-wow
    Tara Browner
My Lord, What a Morning: An Autobiography   *Marian Anderson*
Marian Anderson: A Singer's Journey   *Allan Keiler*
Charles Ives Remembered: An Oral History   *Vivian Perlis*
Henry Cowell, Bohemian   *Michael Hicks*
Rap Music and Street Consciousness   *Cheryl L. Keyes*
Louis Prima   *Garry Boulard*
Marian McPartland's Jazz World: All in Good Time   *Marian McPartland*
Robert Johnson: Lost and Found   *Barry Lee Pearson and Bill McCulloch*
Bound for America: Three British Composers   *Nicholas Temperley*
Lost Sounds: Blacks and the Birth of the Recording Industry, 1890–1919
    Tim Brooks
Burn, Baby! BURN! The Autobiography of Magnificent Montague
    Magnificent Montague with Bob Baker
Way Up North in Dixie: A Black Family's Claim to the Confederate
    Anthem   *Howard L. Sacks and Judith Rose Sacks*
The Bluegrass Reader   *Edited by Thomas Goldsmith*
Colin McPhee: Composer in Two Worlds   *Carol J. Oja*
Robert Johnson, Mythmaking, and Contemporary American Culture
    Patricia R. Schroeder
Composing a World: Lou Harrison, Musical Wayfarer   *Leta E. Miller*
    and Fredric Lieberman
Fritz Reiner, Maestro and Martinet   *Kenneth Morgan*
That Toddlin' Town: Chicago's White Dance Bands and Orchestras, 1900–1950
    Charles A. Sengstock Jr.
Dewey and Elvis: The Life and Times of a Rock 'n' Roll Deejay   *Louis Cantor*
Come Hither to Go Yonder: Playing Bluegrass with Bill Monroe   *Bob Black*
Chicago Blues: Portraits and Stories   *David Whiteis*

The Incredible Band of John Philip Sousa   *Paul E. Bierley*
"Maximum Clarity" and Other Writings on Music   *Ben Johnston,*
   edited by Bob Gilmore
Staging Tradition: John Lair and Sarah Gertrude Knott   *Michael Ann Williams*
Homegrown Music: Discovering Bluegrass   *Stephanie P. Ledgin*
Tales of a Theatrical Guru   *Danny Newman*
The Music of Bill Monroe   *Neil V. Rosenberg and Charles K. Wolfe*
Pressing On: The Roni Stoneman Story   *Roni Stoneman, as told to Ellen Wright*
Together Let Us Sweetly Live   *Jonathan C. David,*
   with photographs by Richard Holloway
Live Fast, Love Hard: The Faron Young Story   *Diane Diekman*
Air Castle of the South: WSM Radio and the Making of Music City
   Craig P. Havighurst
Traveling Home: Sacred Harp Singing and American Pluralism   *Kiri Miller*
Where Did Our Love Go? The Rise and Fall of the Motown Sound   *Nelson George*
Lonesome Cowgirls and Honky-Tonk Angels: The Women of Barn Dance
   Radio   *Kristine M. McCusker*
California Polyphony: Ethnic Voices, Musical Crossroads   *Mina Yang*
The Never-Ending Revival: Rounder Records and the Folk Alliance
   Michael F. Scully
Sing It Pretty: A Memoir   *Bess Lomax Hawes*
Working Girl Blues: The Life and Music of Hazel Dickens   *Hazel Dickens*
   and Bill C. Malone
Charles Ives Reconsidered   *Gayle Sherwood Magee*
The Hayloft Gang: The Story of the National Barn Dance   *Edited by Chad Berry*
Country Music Humorists and Comedians   *Loyal Jones*
Record Makers and Breakers: Voices of the Independent Rock 'n' Roll
   Pioneers   *John Broven*
Music of the First Nations: Tradition and Innovation in Native North
   America   *Edited by Tara Browner*
Cafe Society: The Wrong Place for the Right People   *Barney Josephson,*
   with Terry Trilling-Josephson
George Gershwin: An Intimate Portrait   *Walter Rimler*
Life Flows On in Endless Song: Folk Songs and American History   *Robert V. Wells*
I Feel a Song Coming On: The Life of Jimmy McHugh   *Alyn Shipton*
King of the Queen City: The Story of King Records   *Jon Hartley Fox*
Long Lost Blues: Popular Blues in America, 1850–1920   *Peter C. Muir*
Hard Luck Blues: Roots Music Photographs from the Great Depression
   Rich Remsberg
Restless Giant: The Life and Times of Jean Aberbach and Hill and Range Songs
   Bar Biszick-Lockwood
Champagne Charlie and Pretty Jemima: Variety Theater in the Nineteenth Century
   Gillian M. Rodger
Sacred Steel: Inside an African American Steel Guitar Tradition   *Robert L. Stone*

Gone to the Country: The New Lost City Ramblers and the Folk Music Revival
    Ray Allen
The Makers of the Sacred Harp   *David Warren Steel with Richard H. Hulan*
Woody Guthrie, American Radical   *Will Kaufman*
George Szell: A Life of Music   *Michael Charry*
Bean Blossom: The Brown County Jamboree and Bill Monroe's Bluegrass
    Festivals   *Thomas A. Adler*
Crowe on the Banjo: The Music Life of J. D. Crowe   *Marty Godbey*
Twentieth Century Drifter: The Life of Marty Robbins   *Diane Diekman*
Henry Mancini: Reinventing Film Music   *John Caps*
The Beautiful Music All Around Us: Field Recordings and the American Experience
    Stephen Wade
Then Sings My Soul: The Culture of Southern Gospel Music   *Douglas Harrison*
The Accordion in the Americas: Klezmer, Polka, Tango, Zydeco, and More!
    Edited by Helena Simonett
Bluegrass Bluesman: A Memoir   *Josh Graves, edited by Fred Bartenstein*
One Woman in a Hundred: Edna Phillips and the Philadelphia Orchestra
    Mary Sue Welsh
The Great Orchestrator: Arthur Judson and American Arts Management
    James M. Doering
Charles Ives in the Mirror: American Histories of an Iconic Composer
    David C. Paul
Southern Soul-Blues   *David Whiteis*
Sweet Air: Modernism, Regionalism, and American Popular Song
    Edward P. Comentale
Pretty Good for a Girl: Women in Bluegrass   *Murphy Hicks Henry*
Sweet Dreams: The World of Patsy Cline   *Warren R. Hofstra*
William Sidney Mount and the Creolization of American Culture
    Christopher J. Smith
Bird: The Life and Music of Charlie Parker   *Chuck Haddix*
Making the March King: John Philip Sousa's Washington Years, 1854–1893
    Patrick Warfield
In It for the Long Run   *Jim Rooney*
Pioneers of the Blues Revival   *Steve Cushing*
Roots of the Revival: American and British Folk Music in the 1950s
    Ronald D. Cohen and Rachel Clare Donaldson
Blues All Day Long: The Jimmy Rogers Story   *Wayne Everett Goins*
Yankee Twang: Country and Western Music in New England   *Clifford R. Murphy*
The Music of the Stanley Brothers   *Gary B. Reid*
Hawaiian Music in Motion: Mariners, Missionaries, and Minstrels
    James Revell Carr
Sounds of the New Deal: The Federal Music Project in the West   *Peter Gough*
The Mormon Tabernacle Choir: A Biography   *Michael Hicks*
The Man That Got Away: The Life and Songs of Harold Arlen   *Walter Rimler*
A City Called Heaven: Chicago and the Birth of Gospel Music   *Robert M. Marovich*

Blues Unlimited: Essential Interviews from the Original Blues Magazine
    Edited by Bill Greensmith, Mike Rowe, and Mark Camarigg
Hoedowns, Reels, and Frolics: Roots and Branches of Southern Appalachian
    Dance   *Phil Jamison*
Fannie Bloomfield-Zeisler: The Life and Times of a Piano Virtuoso   *Beth Abelson
    Macleod*
Cybersonic Arts: Adventures in American New Music   *Gordon Mumma,
    edited with commentary by Michelle Fillion*
The Magic of Beverly Sills   *Nancy Guy*
Waiting for Buddy Guy   *Alan Harper*
Harry T. Burleigh: From the Spiritual to the Harlem Renaissance   *Jean E. Snyder*
Music in the Age of Anxiety: American Music in the Fifties   *James Wierzbicki*
Jazzing: New York City's Unseen Scene   *Thomas H. Greenland*
A Cole Porter Companion   *Edited by Don M. Randel, Matthew Shaftel,
    and Susan Forscher Weiss*
Foggy Mountain Troubadour: The Life and Music of Curly Seckler   *Penny Parsons*
Blue Rhythm Fantasy: Big Band Jazz Arranging in the Swing Era   *John Wriggle*
Bill Clifton: America's Bluegrass Ambassador to the World   *Bill C. Malone*
Chinatown Opera Theater in North America   *Nancy Yunhwa Rao*
The Elocutionists: Women, Music, and the Spoken Word   *Marian Wilson Kimber*
May Irwin: Singing, Shouting, and the Shadow of Minstrelsy   *Sharon Ammen*
Peggy Seeger: A Life of Music, Love, and Politics   *Jean R. Freedman*
Charles Ives's *Concord*: Essays after a Sonata   *Kyle Gann*
Don't Give Your Heart to a Rambler: My Life with Jimmy Martin, the King
    of Bluegrass   *Barbara Martin Stephens*
Libby Larsen: Composing an American Life   *Denise Von Glahn*
George Szell's Reign: Behind the Scenes with the Cleveland Orchestra
    Marcia Hansen Kraus
Just One of the Boys: Female-to-Male Cross-Dressing on the American Variety
    Stage   *Gillian M. Rodger*
Spirituals and the Birth of a Black Entertainment Industry   *Sandra Jean Graham*
Right to the Juke Joint: A Personal History of American Music   *Patrick B. Mullen*
Bluegrass Generation: A Memoir   *Neil V. Rosenberg*
Pioneers of the Blues Revival, Expanded Second Edition   *Steve Cushing*
Banjo Roots and Branches   *Edited by Robert Winans*
Bill Monroe: The Life and Music of the Blue Grass Man   *Tom Ewing*
Dixie Dewdrop: The Uncle Dave Macon Story   *Michael D. Doubler*
Los Romeros: Royal Family of the Spanish Guitar   *Walter Aaron Clark*
Transforming Women's Education: Liberal Arts and Music in Female
    Seminaries   *Jewel A. Smith*
Rethinking American Music   *Edited by Tara Browner and Thomas L. Riis*
Leonard Bernstein and the Language of Jazz   *Katherine Baber*
Dancing Revolution: Bodies, Space, and Sound in American Cultural History
    Christopher J. Smith
Peggy Glanville-Hicks: Composer and Critic   *Suzanne Robinson*
Mormons, Musical Theater, and Belonging in America   *Jake Johnson*

Blues Legacy: Tradition and Innovation in Chicago   *David Whiteis*
Blues before Sunrise 2: Interviews from the Chicago Scene   *Steve Cushing*
The Cashaway Psalmody: Transatlantic Religion and Music in Colonial Carolina
   Stephen A. Marini
Earl Scruggs and Foggy Mountain Breakdown: The Making of an American Classic
   Thomas Goldsmith
A Guru's Journey: Pandit Chitresh Das and Indian Classical Dance in
   Diaspora   *Sarah Morelli*
Unsettled Scores: Politics, Hollywood, and the Film Music of Aaron Copland and
   Hanns Eisler   *Sally Bick*
Hillbilly Maidens, Okies, and Cowgirls: Women's Country Music, 1930–1960
   Stephanie Vander Wel
Always the Queen: The Denise LaSalle Story   *Denise LaSalle with David Whiteis*
Artful Noise: Percussion Literature in the Twentieth Century   *Thomas Siwe*
The Heart of a Woman: The Life and Music of Florence B. Price   *Rae Linda Brown,*
   edited by Guthrie P. Ramsey Jr.
When Sunday Comes: Gospel Music in the Soul and Hip-Hop Eras
   Claudrena N. Harold
The Lady Swings: Memoirs of a Jazz Drummer   *Dottie Dodgion and Wayne Enstice*
Industrial Strength Bluegrass: Southwestern Ohio's Musical Legacy
   Edited by Fred Bartenstein and Curtis W. Ellison
Soul on Soul: The Life and Music of Mary Lou Williams   *Tammy L. Kernodle*
Unbinding Gentility: Women Making Music in the Nineteenth-Century South
   Candace Bailey
Punks in Peoria: Making a Scene in the American Heartland   *Jonathan Wright*
   and Dawson Barrett
Homer Rodeheaver and the Rise of the Gospel Music Industry   *Kevin Mungons*
   and Douglas Yeo
Americanaland: Where Country & Western Met Rock 'n' Roll   *John Milward,*
   with portraits by Margie Greve
Listening to Bob Dylan   *Larry Starr*
Lying in the Middle: Musical Theater and Belief at the Heart of America
   Jake Johnson
The Sounds of Place: Music and the American Cultural Landscape
   Denise Von Glahn
Peace Be Still: How James Cleveland and the Angelic Choir Created a Gospel Classic
   Robert M. Marovich
Politics as Sound: The Washington, DC, Hardcore Scene, 1978–1983
   Shayna L. Maskell
Tania León's Stride: A Polyrhythmic Life   *Alejandro L. Madrid*
Elliott Carter Speaks: Unpublished Lectures   *Elliott Carter, edited by Laura Emmery*
Interviews with American Composers: Barney Childs in Conversation
   Barney Childs, edited by Virginia Anderson
Queer Country   *Shana Goldin-Perschbacher*
On the Bus with Bill Monroe: My Five-Year Ride with the Father of Blue Grass
   Mark Hembree

The University of Illinois Press
is a founding member of the
Association of University Presses.

_____

Composed in 10.25/14 Chaparral Pro
with Amber Whiskey and DIN 1451 Std display
by Lisa Connery
at the University of Illinois Press
Manufactured by Sheridan Books, Inc.

University of Illinois Press
1325 South Oak Street
Champaign, IL 61820-6903
www.press.uillinois.edu